STEADY
THE
SHIP

Encouragement as the
Day Draws Near

Kristen Michelle

Published by KHARIS PUBLISHING, imprint of KHARIS MEDIA LLC.

Copyright © 2021 Kristen Michelle

ISBN-13: 978-1-63746-074-0

ISBN-10: 1-63746-074-0

Library of Congress Control Number: 2021943373

Cover Photo by: Spratt, Annie. On deck of the Opal Schooner with North Sailing. Greenland & the Arctic, https://unsplash.com.

Dedication Graphic by: Derbisheva, Yuliya. Watercolor eucalyptus branch wreath. Stock Illustrations | Paint 1138432594, www.istockphoto.com.

Dedication Photo by: Michelle, Kristen. Photo of Letters. July 2020. Author's personal collection.

All KHARIS PUBLISHING products are available at special quantity discounts for bulk purchase for sales promotions, premiums, fund-raising, and educational needs. For details, contact:

Kharis Media LLC
Tel: 1-479-599-8657
support@kharispublishing.com
www.kharispublishing.com

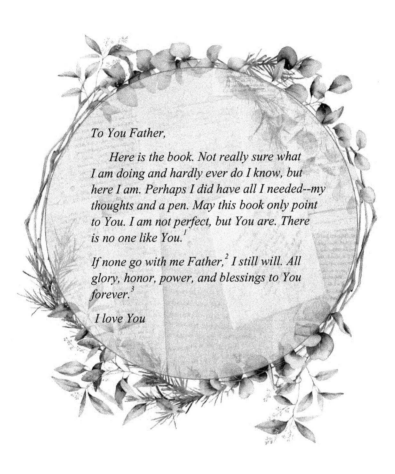

To You Father,

Here is the book. Not really sure what I am doing and hardly ever do I know, but here I am. Perhaps I did have all I needed--my thoughts and a pen. May this book only point to You. I am not perfect, but You are. There is no one like You.[1]

If none go with me Father,[2] I still will. All glory, honor, power, and blessings to You forever.[3]

I love You

Thank you, Kharis Publishing, my editor Mrs. Karen, my attorney Mrs. Vedia, my friends and family and, most importantly, thank You Holy Spirit. Thank you all for helping me.

EDITOR'S NOTE

Kristen Michelle comes straight from the heart in bringing the scriptures to life and applying them to our daily lives and current reality. They are not just ancient words to reflect upon but living, breathing advice we can rely upon whether we experience pain or joy. These are timeless, fundamental truths, and Kristen gifts them to us in fresh and relevant ways.

Steady the Ship gives us a wonderful image grounded in biblical imagery that is pertinent to the current state of the world and our place in it. We learn that Kristen has found that suffering has brought forth revelations of deep inner truths and newly found strength. She knows that for each one of us that strength does not come from our will or ego but from the ultimate source of creation and truth. She doesn't shy away from asking probing, personal questions of God. That is a huge step in fostering an intimate relationship with the Creator. She doesn't rely on intermediaries or interpreters but rather goes right to the source, the scriptures, and seeks direct answers. While clear explanations and responses are not always forthcoming to us, it is more important that we make the approach and express the emotions we feel when encountering challenges and difficulties in our life. There is comfort in Kristen's honest and forthright manner of simply crying out and expressing those feelings of sadness and confusion that are familiar to all of us. Her words are at once intensely personal and profoundly universal.

Interestingly, there were many times when editing this book that I questioned Kristen's mode of expression. She responded with an open mind and deep humility. However, she also insisted on maintaining her own voice—not in a strict literary sense but from a place of genuine expression and yearning. To sanitize those words would only serve to extract the individuality and unique ways in which she reaches out to the reader and touches us with her authenticity and uncensored passion for her faith and her desire to share it.

Editing *Steady the Ship* was often an emotional experience for me, sometimes bringing me to tears with its plaintive cries and acceptance of the unknowable. Faith, after all, is the ability to trust what cannot be seen and to rely on our connection to God. Kristen has found that strong, instinctive anchor for her ship that serves as a loving guide for us to do the same.

—**Karen Corinne Herceg,** Author, Poet, Editor

CONTENTS

GREETINGS

Job 7:7 (NASB) "Remember that my life is *but* breath; my eye will not again see good.

Mark 1:17 And Jesus said to them, "Follow Me, and I will make you become fishers of men."

Genesis 8:11 The dove came to him toward evening, and behold, in her beak was a freshly picked olive leaf. So Noah knew that the water was abated from the earth.

Colossians 3:2-3 Set your mind on the things above, not on the things that are on earth. For you have died and your life is hidden with Christ in God.

Hebrews 10:24-25 and let us consider how to stimulate one another to love and good deeds, not forsaking our own assembling together, as is the habit of some, but encouraging *one another;* and all the more as you see the day drawing near.

To the Reader

I am but a breath[1] somewhere on the timeline of the history of life, where the fishing industry abounds. A few of us are sailing across the open sea with a destination in mind. The only way to get to where we are going is to navigate these waters with our small ship and raising our sails with their halyard lines. Our journey on this worn, torn, and aging fishing vessel has had some ups and downs. Some days have been good, some not so much. Some days have been clear blue skies and sun rays, and some dark with our ship fighting against the wind and waves. As the storms come and go, it seems to be getting harder to hang on to hope.

Some days when the storm is raging with the sea crashing over the deck, we feel as though we are drowning. It is uncertain how much time is left until we get to where we are going. For now, it is just another heartache, another crash, another day in our journey.

As I sit in the cabin and write this in my journal, I am trying to hold onto the faith that it won't always be like this. The faith where this sadness and despair disappear. If only there would be a sign that our destination is just over the horizon, in way of the shore we would steer... Great, the boat is battling another breaking wave and things are falling down on the floor again. It is hard when things are always thrown at you, things out of your control, it seems to never end. I guess I will pick everything up--again. As I pick up the stuff scattered amongst the planks, I notice a book lying there. I dust it off and open it to see what it says. I can't believe it. It reads:

> *I know we do not know each other, and I do not know what moment in life this is for you, or what season in life you are in. But nonetheless, I hope you are okay. Sometimes the waters in the sea (life) can be overwhelming, making it hard to breathe, but know that you are not alone. There are others of us trying to navigate our ship through these waters too, steering towards home. The Son is near [2] even when you can't see. He will never leave or forsake you[3] no matter how bad the waters may seem. I pray for the breath for this moment, for the reality of your faith,[4] and for morning to come fast, so there is a new day and new mercies.[5] It will not always hurt this way my friend, the waters will recede.*

This book you are holding is full of letters, some exploring who the Creator (Father) is, some of wonder, vulnerability, thanksgiving, encouragement, and pain, all on a page. I hope they take you outside of the space and place you are in and speak to you in the way you need. For the one who feels as if they are drowning, don't give up or grow weary because good is coming. No matter if it is by or large, you have to keep going. I hope these letters encourage you to steady the ship of your mind, arch the bow of your heart (your spirit), and take hold of the Hand already taking hold of you. May your dove find an olive leaf of hope as the waters recede.[6]

I wonder how sometimes I hear exactly what I need, even if the waves do drop the words right in front of me. I think I am going to put my journal away, sit back, and continue to read.

Until next time. – Passenger of the Colossians 3:2.

P.S. Reader, might we spur one another on[7] as we navigate the waters of this life, until we reach the promised land,[8] where our hearts will never fail again.

--**Kristen**

FATHER

CHAPTER 1

The Book

Romans 10:8-10 But what does it say? "THE WORD IS NEAR YOU, IN YOUR MOUTH AND IN YOUR HEART" --that is, the word of faith which we are preaching, that if you confess with your mouth Jesus *as* Lord, and believe in your heart that God raised Him from the dead, you will be saved; for with the heart a person believes, resulting in righteousness, and with the mouth he confesses, resulting in salvation.

2 Corinthians 1:3-4 Blessed *be* the God and Father of our Lord Jesus Christ, the Father of mercies and God of all comfort, who comforts us in all our affliction so that we will be able to comfort those who are in any affliction with the comfort with which we ourselves are comforted by God.

Ephesians 6:16-17 in addition to all, taking up the shield of faith with which you will be able to extinguish all the flaming arrows of the evil *one*. And take THE HELMET OF SALVATION, and the sword of the Spirit, which is the word of God.

John 3:8 The wind blows where it wishes and you hear the sound of it, but do not know where it comes from and where it is going; so is everyone who is born of the Spirit."

Psalm 118:21 I shall give thanks to You, for You have answered me, and You have become my salvation.

The Book

Father, Jesus, Holy Spirit,

Thank You.

I ask for the one who is reading this if their needs could be met, along with their families, friends, and animals, too. Could their hearts accept You are real if they have not before? Father, I pray for the person who is having a hard day. Could You wrap them up into You and breathe for them? Father, since faith is the reality of what is hoped for,[1] please could You give them what they have had faith for? Could they fall asleep and rest easy as the new day comes fast with Your new mercies?[2] Thank You.

It has been a long journey, where I feel as if I have been stuck in a field alone planting my seeds of hope. I have been wondering if this was Your way of showing me how to use my bow and arrows. Where I would learn how to fight the giants on my own like David, when the enemy shouts at me.[3] Where I could start to see all the weeds the enemy tries to plant[4] meant to choke out my hope; and know how to cut them down with the sharpest two-edged Sword,[5] so I can stand my ground and see my hope-seeds grow. Whatever the reason for the long journey alone, I hope I have been doing what You planned. I do not understand the reason for this book, but I really hope the person in whose hands You place this knows You are real, You love them, and there is hope. I ask for sustainment for them and encouragement to keep going, no matter how excruciating it feels, because we never know when one of our hope-seeds will start growing in our field.

Please could You keep guiding me as You do and take me wherever we are going?[6] Thank You for all You have done and are doing.

I love You.

P.S. Father could You help my seeds to germinate and grow?

CHAPTER 2

You

Acts 17:24-25 The God who made the world and all things in it, since He is Lord of heaven and earth, does not dwell in temples made with hands; nor is He served by human hands, as though He needed anything, since He Himself gives to all *people* life and breath and all things;

1 John 3:20 in whatever our heart condemns us; for God is greater than our heart and knows all things.

1 Timothy 1:17 Now to the King eternal, immortal, invisible, the only God, *be* honor and glory forever and ever. Amen.

Psalm 135:6 Whatever the LORD pleases, He does, in heaven and in earth, in the seas and in all deeps.

Psalm 71:15 My mouth shall tell of Your righteousness *and* of Your salvation all day long; for I do not know the sum *of them*.

You

Father, Jesus, Holy Spirit,

Thank You.

Father, who are You whom I love? Sometimes, honestly, I cannot understand You, whether it is Your nature, what You look like, or why You do the things You do. Even how You have already read my letter, but I haven't written it yet. The most difficult thing for me to understand is how You came to be, because You didn't. You just have always been. So, who are You? In Your Book I see it says You are the Creator of all things,[1] You are the only God,[2] You made us and we are Yours,[3] You are our Father and Father of our spirits.[4] You are perfect,[5] and Your word is pure.[6] You are the King of the nations,[7] King of glory,[8] the Lord of Armies,[9] and Watcher of humanity.[10] The God of Abraham, Isaac, and Jacob.[11] You are the Rock,[12] the Rock of Israel,[13] the God of Israel.[14]

You are love. You are patient and kind. Love does not envy, is not boastful or conceited, does not act improperly, is not selfish, and is not provoked. You do not keep a record of wrongs for those who are Yours. You find no joy in unrighteousness, and You rejoice in the truth. Love bears all things, believes all things, hopes all things, and endures all things. You never end. You are good, faithful, gentle, and humble in heart.[15-27]

Father this isn't even half of what Your words say You are. It also says You are: forgiving, gracious, compassionate, slow to anger, merciful, righteous, great, mighty, awesome, awe inspiring, glorious, light, consuming fire, jealous, avenging, strong, wise, all knowing, all powerful, great in power, everywhere, unchangeable, a shield, a soft whisper, restoring, healing, and encouraging. You are the God of endurance, hope, peace, truth, of all grace, of all comfort, Father of mercies, our Savior and Redeemer. You love righteousness, justice, and will not abandon Your faithful ones. You are the Almighty, the Majesty, the Majestic Glory, the Holy One, the Eternal One, the Everlasting God, the Alpha and Omega, the One who is, who was, who is coming, and You are--I Am.[28-74]

So then, what do You look like? Your letters say You are Spirit. What does a spirit look like? You say we are made in Your image and likeness, we reflect Your glory, and we are being transformed into the same image. Your letters also say Jesus took on the likeness of men and came as a man in His external form. Does this mean our internal form is our spirit, and our spirit is what is being transformed? In Your letters there are moments when You are spoken of with human features, like Your face, eyes, pupil, ears, mouth, nostrils, heart, arm, hand, back, and feet.[75-90]

Do You really have these features or are they written so we can understand what You are saying, or maybe both? What about those times You appear as different things like a burning bush,[91] a cloud,[92] or a fire?[93] What about the references of Your feathers[94] and wings,[95] and all the visions of You on Your throne.[96] Father, how can these things be? Because Your letters also say You are invisible[97] and no one has ever seen You?[98] I used to think no one had ever seen You because You didn't want them to see You. But could it be the reason no one has ever seen You (except Jesus because He is You)[99]--is it as simple as You are invisible? Are You invisible but You manifest Yourself into things so we can see You are there? Or do You allow us to see the glory coming from You? (Your letters talk about the many times You have appeared to people. It would be neat to see all the ways You have appeared). When You say the upright will see Your face,[100] and the little one's angels see Your face continually in Heaven,[101] is this Jesus' face? It is hard for me to think through and comprehend this. I have always imagined You sitting on Your throne as a big and mighty being, with me hiding behind and hugging Your leg, or just sitting in Your lap. Maybe You are these things for me with human features when I need it, and are a fire or cloud when I need those too, because You supply all my needs?[102]

I do not think my letter is capturing all of who You are; there is so much to You. Job talked a lot about what You have done and said those were just the fringes of Your ways.[103] I feel like what I have written down so far are just the fringes of who You are.

Father there are some things I know and have realized about You, like how You made all of us on purpose and You love and care for us. You are timeless and don't go out of style. You make things known; You give to us and comfort us. You judge, guide, save, protect, and give second chances. You fight for us, search for us, teach and discipline us, and provide for us. All of this You do even for just one, and You have done so for me. Like

8

David said, You have crowned me with love and compassion. Thank You. You are good and great![104-121]

So, Father, with all the wondering and all the searching I have done about who You are and what You look like, I have come to the conclusion that You can look and be whatever You want to be, when You want to be it, displaying Your ability. Whether You sit,[122] stand,[123] walk,[124] fly on the wings of the wind,[125] hover,[126] blow,[127] shine,[128] take on human features, show Your glory, or just be invisible. Which brings me to another conclusion: the reason my words can't capture all of who You are is because I can't sum Someone up who Is, because You are…because You just Are. You are the One,[129] the true One.[130] The Ancient of Days.[131] There is no one like You,[132] the only wise,[133] Most High,[134] immortal,[135] living God.[136] Yahweh is Your name.[137] The Lord is Your name,[138] and You Are who I love.

I love You.

P.S. I see why You told Moses to tell the Israelites "I AM has sent me to you."[139]

CHAPTER 3

The Name

John 1:18 (CSB) No one has ever seen God. The one and only Son, who is himself God and is at the Father's side —he has revealed him.

Psalm 103:10-13 He has not dealt with us according to our sins, nor rewarded us according to our iniquities. For as high as the heavens are above the earth, so great is His lovingkindness toward those who fear Him. As far as the east is from the west, so far has He removed our transgressions from us. Just as a father has compassion on *his* children, so the LORD has compassion on those who fear Him.

Matthew 26:67-68 Then they spat in His face and beat Him with their fists; and others slapped Him, and said, "Prophesy to us, You Christ; who is the one who hit You?"

Luke 22:49-51 When those who were around Him saw what was going to happen, they said, "Lord, shall we strike with the sword?" And one of them struck the slave of the high priest and cut off his right ear. But Jesus answered and said, "Stop! No more of this." And He touched his ear and healed him.

Matthew 16:16 Simon Peter answered, "You are the Christ, the Son of the living God."

The Name

Father, Jesus, Holy Spirit,

Thank You.

Hi Jesus, I am writing this letter just for You. All these letters are for You as well because not only are You Jesus, but You are Father too.[1] This is hard to comprehend for me sometimes, how You, Father and Holy Spirit, are three in one.[2] Even though I can't quite comprehend right now how You are You, but also two other beings, I go with it because You say so. You also say I am Your sister.[3] Sometimes when I think of You, I think of You as my big brother protecting me and watching out for me. You are so very kind to me, compassionate towards me, and I do not deserve You. I do, say, and think things I wish I didn't, and I used to think I should just go to Hell anyway because I do not deserve to be in Your presence. Then I learned later I shouldn't think this either, because even though I don't deserve You, it does not change what You did on the cross[4] and what it means. All I can do is accept that Your love covers me and gives me what I don't deserve --Your grace.[5] Thank You for reclining at the table with me.[6]

Jesus, You knew we would need help as we struggled here on earth, so Father sent You.[7] You sent Yourself, knowing You were going to have to go through the pain. As a matter of fact, one of the nails that hurt you was my fault; instead of them putting the nail in my hand, You had them put it in Your hand. I hate this. I hate that I caused You pain.

How did You walk beside us on earth knowing in advance we would betray You,[8] deny You,[9] spit on You,[10] hit You in Your face,[11] and make fun of who You are?[12] When You hung there on the wood *You* created[13] and we humans made into a cross and nailed You to it,[14] with your flesh hanging off and Your blood dripping to the ground, how were You not mad with us? I said once I wanted to have the greatest love story, and a friend with such kindness told me there already was the greatest love story,[15] and it was You. She was right.

So why do people get so upset at Your name Jesus? You came to help them! You came to help me. You rescued me and set me free from my sins[16] so I could be with You. You have caught my heart every time it has been

13

stomped on, tossed away, and beaten down. You showed me the way out of the pit[17] when I was pushed into it and made a way every time there was not supposed to be one. You have comforted me when I cried[18] and gave me hope when there wasn't any. If only I could just hug You. I don't know how You do it, how You can be there for everyone all at the same time even when You go after the one.[19] How You make impossible things happen,[20] even how You healed the ear of someone who was coming to seize You,[21] or how You can comfort me when my heart hurts because I hurt You.

I guess it is just because You Are He. The Overseer of our souls. You are the Chief Shepherd and the Lamb, You are Man and God, The Word, The Light, Seed, The True Vine, The Branch, The Bread, The Way, The Truth, The Life, the Root and descendant of David, the Bright Morning Star, Wonderful Counselor, Mighty God, Eternal Father, Prince of Peace, Lord of lords, King of kings, Resurrection and the Life, Victorious, the Holy and Righteous One, the Beloved One, the Amen, the faithful and true Witness, the Originator of God's creation, the Lord of glory, You are the Alpha and Omega, the First and the Last, the Beginning and the End. [22-43]

Jesus Christ, You are the Name.[44] Thank You that I have life in Your name,[45] You are the *only* way to Father.[46] You are the gate.[47] Yours is[48] because You Are! You are the best forever!

I love You.

P.S. I say You are the Messiah, the Son of the living God.[49]

CHAPTER 4

Greater Are You

Galatians 4:6 Because you are sons, God has sent forth the Spirit of His Son into our hearts, crying, "Abba! Father!"

Romans 8:23 And not only this, but also we ourselves, having the first fruits of the Spirit, even we ourselves groan within ourselves, waiting eagerly for *our* adoption as sons, the redemption of our body.

Ephesians 6:17 And take THE HELMET OF SALVATION, and the sword of the Spirit, which is the word of God.

Job 33:4 "The Spirit of God has made me, and the breath of the Almighty gives me life.

1 John 4:4 You are from God, little children, and have overcome them; because greater is He who is in you than he who is in the world.

Greater Are You

Father, Jesus, Holy Spirit,

Thank You.

Genesis 1:1-2 "In the beginning God created the heavens and the earth. Now the earth was formless and empty, darkness covered the surface of the watery depths, and the Spirit of God was hovering over the surface of the waters."

Holy Spirit, along with Father and Jesus, You have been since the beginning. You are the Spirit of Father and Jesus.[1] You are Holy,[2] the Spirit of holiness,[3] Spirit of glory,[4] Spirit of truth,[5] Spirit of grace,[6] Spirit of wisdom and understanding, Spirit of counsel and strength, Spirit of knowledge and fear of the Lord.[7] You are Power,[8] the Counselor,[9] the good Spirit,[10] Promised Spirit,[11] eternal Spirit,[12] and You give life.[13] For those of us whose beings believed, we are sealed with You.[14] You were given as a down payment to us for what is to come.[15] You fill our hearts and cause us to flow with living water[16] and to cry out: "Abba, Father".[17] Because of You, we know our story does not end here on this earth, but yet the place which is being prepared for us[18] awaits.

When You were hovering over the earth when it was formless and empty, did You think about how one day the formless and empty place would be filled with Your creation, Your breath, Your chosen ones, You and me? Were You eagerly waiting for my inner being to accept You so You could come be with me, where now I eagerly wait?[19] Did You think about this moment where I would want to write this letter to You? Or did You think about how the fire I would have to go through would show me more of You, because I would draw near?[20] That I would realize You had been there all along, and there is more to You than what I didn't understand about You?

Your Sword, which is sharper than any two-edged sword,[21] says You made me,[22] and Father's breath gave me life.[23] It is as if You created me, saved me, renewed me, gave me a Guide to read that speaks in so many different ways, and also gave me access to a 24-hour support line: You. Thank You that no matter where I go my heart is touching You. No matter *what*

17

direction I go, there You are.[24] It seems like it must be true that I am never alone if where I go, then there You are?

When I sit back and take a moment… and think… about how the Creator,[25] Authority of all,[26] the Holy One,[27] the Perfect One,[28] the One who is praised nonstop,[29] the King,[30] His Spirit, You, You choose to dwell within me? Right here in this moment and every other moment, You live inside of me?[31] All this power, All this peace, All that is lovely, All that is worthy of all creation's praise, I am Your temple?[32]

Is this what they call an inside connection? This must explain some of the weird and neat things which have happened in my life. There have been way too many specific coincidences, perfectly timed situations, promptings which didn't make sense until obeyed, things that showed up out of nowhere, knowledge given not taught by human wisdom, a specific word for the specific moment, strength, convictions, teachings, revelations, leading, guiding, reminding, testifying, comfort in the most horrific situations, where to go, what to do, what to say, and when to say it. Jesus said just like we do not know where the wind comes from or where it is going, so it is with us who have You.[33-44] The possibilities are endless. I cannot live this life without You. Even though I do not know where You are taking me, I would still rather be with You and not know, then do life alone and not have You to go with me.

I see how You are a gift,[45] and I am so thankful for You and how You help me. I am sorry when I ignore promptings or do things You so gently tell me not to do. I do not know why I do this sometimes, because I just want to please You. Thank You for your patience with me, for interceding for me,[46] for helping me in so many ways. Thank You for telling me not to listen when the enemy starts to babble, thank You for the gifts You give,[47] thank You that there is freedom here with You,[48] and thank You for being here with me.

Holy Spirit, one of my favorite prompting moments You gave to me shows me how gentle You are, but also how great You are; how You care for the small things, even some of the smallest of Your creation. Thank You for allowing me to still remember this moment. I never knew something so small could be so special to me. I hope I never forget. I hope I never forget the day I was cleaning the house and I saw something out of the corner of my eye, out of the back door when I walked by it. Something had fallen and landed on the concrete patio. I did not look or pay any attention to what it was and just went on cleaning. Then I just had this feeling, it had to be You, this feeling I needed to go back and see what it was, just to go see. So, I stopped what I was doing and went to look. There was a butterfly sitting there on the patio. In many ways this wasn't a big deal, because I had seen a bunch of butterflies already. For some reason the back part of my house that year was the gathering place for tons of caterpillars who made their cocoons there, (which when I look back on this now, how amazing that was). Also, it was just a butterfly, why did I feel like I needed to go look at another butterfly? But isn't that just it? Sometimes what we think we see actually isn't what we see. When I went outside and looked closer, it wasn't just a butterfly, it was a butterfly that could not fly away after he came out of his cocoon. The wings on one side of its body were crossed making it impossible for him to fly. I knew I was not supposed to touch his wings because it takes their scales off that they need, but I knew he needed help. (I should have realized then that You were going to protect his scales, so it was okay). I was reluctant to touch him, but I reached down and gently uncrossed his wings. Right when I did this, he flew up and landed on my chest for just a moment, and then he flew away as I watched. It was such a special moment to me, and I would have never been able to help him if I hadn't walked by the door at the exact moment he fell, and if I hadn't listened to Your prompting to look and see what it was. Thank You for allowing me to help him. He knew he needed You. How compassionate You are to care for these little things.[49] I am honored to be used to help him.

Thank You for dwelling in me[50] and for showing me love, joy, peace, patience, kindness, goodness, faithfulness, gentleness, and self-control.[51] Greater are You in me than the one in the world.[52] How beautiful and neat You Are. Thank You Holy Spirit for everything, forever.

I love You.

P.S. Thank You for sending that bird over to me today.

CHAPTER 5

Valentine's Day

John 14:27 Peace I leave with you; My peace I give to you; not as the world gives do I give to you. Do not let your heart be troubled, nor let it be fearful.

1 Kings 8:60 so that all the peoples of the earth may know that the LORD is God; there is no one else.

John 15:12-15 "This is My commandment, that you love one another, just as I have loved you. Greater love has no one than this, that one lay down his life for his friends. You are My friends if you do what I command you. No longer do I call you slaves, for the slave does not know what his master is doing; but I have called you friends, for all things that I have heard from My Father I have made known to you.

Mark 10:16 And He took them in His arms and *began* blessing them, laying His hands on them.

John 16:16 "A little while, and you will no longer see Me; and again a little while, and you will see Me."

Valentine's Day

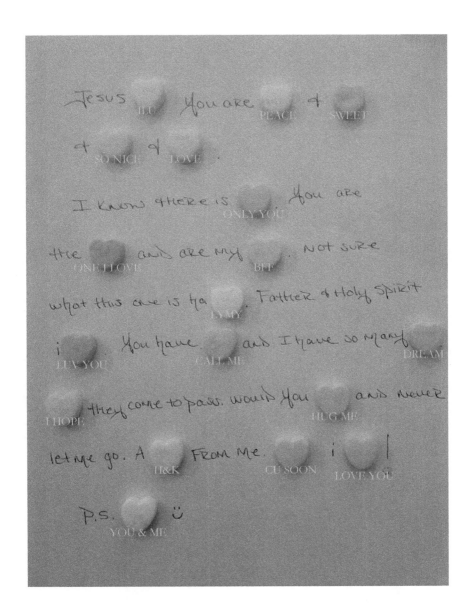

Jesus [ILU] You are [PEACE] + [SWEET] + [SO NICE] + [LOVE].

I know there is [ONLY YOU] You are the [ONE I LOVE] and are my [BFF]. Not sure what this are is ha [IN MY]. Father & Holy spirit i [LUV YOU]. You have [CALL ME] and I have so many [DREAM] [I HOPE] they come to pass. would you [HUG ME] and never let me go. A [H&K] From me. [CU SOON] i [LOVE YOU] |

P.S. [YOU & ME] ☺

CHAPTER 6

Thank You

1 Thessalonians 5:18 in everything give thanks; for this is God's will for you in Christ Jesus.

Psalm 86:5 For You, Lord, are good, and ready to forgive, and abundant in lovingkindness to all who call upon You.

Proverbs 17:22 A joyful heart is good medicine, but a broken spirit dries up the bones.

Isaiah 55:10 "For as the rain and the snow come down from heaven, and do not return there without watering the earth and making it bear and sprout, and furnishing seed to the sower and bread to the eater;

Proverbs 3:19-20 The LORD by wisdom founded the earth, by understanding He established the heavens. By His knowledge the deeps were broken up and the skies drip with dew.

Thank You

Father, Jesus, Holy Spirit,

Thank You.

Hi, Father. Thank You for the food I am eating right now; it is good. Thank You for it being available to buy and for giving me the ability to buy it. Thank You for the person or people who made it. Wherever they are right now, I ask that they could be having a good day, their needs could be met, they could know You are real, and they could have a blessing today.

Father, I am sorry for all the times when I come to You with requests and I do not thank You first. This is why I started to always put "Thank You" at the beginning of all my letters, to thank You for everything, and to remind myself to always have a posture of thanksgiving[1] because You are good.

Thank You for You being You. For being love,[2] being nice and kind to me, even when I am not kind to You. For being here with me, always helping me, being patient with me, giving me grace I never deserve, being my Father, and being my Friend. Thank You for creating us, saving us, and helping us. Thank You for Your angels, for their help and protection. You did not have to do any of this; You are good.

You didn't have to create us and give us these bodies, but You decided to do so. Your Word says You saw all You had made and it was very good.[3] Thank You for knitting us together[4] and covering our bones with tendons, flesh, and skin,[5] and breathing life into us.[6] Thank You for how our bone marrow, where Your Word penetrates,[7] makes two million new blood cells a second.[8] For how the blood flows continuously in the right path, and flows in single lines.[9] For how the heart, creating its own electrical system,[10] can get blood to all areas of our body through thousands of miles of blood vessels and can pump over 2000 gallons of blood a day.[11] How our bodies automatically breathe in oxygen filtering and cleaning it. (It is neat how we inhale oxygen and exhale CO_2 while plants take in CO_2 and give off oxygen).[12] How our brains have around a 100 billion neurons sending information back and forth, with each one of those neurons having the ability to make tens of thousands of connections.[13] How our nervous system is able to receive and send between 10 and 500 electrical impulses per second to help our bodies make decisions.[14] How the digestive system with a 20-foot-long small intestine breaks down food so nutrients can be absorbed.[15] How our immune system has three lines of defense to protect itself.[16] How the body can heal and restore itself in so many ways including fasting,[17] sleeping where cells repair themselves and growth hormones increase that help rebuild bones and muscles,[18] and laughter helping our heart by relaxing our blood vessels, lowering stress hormones and raising good cholesterol.[19] For our bones that are as strong as cast iron that protect our organs and for how they store and help maintain the right amount of calcium and phosphorus.[20] For our 40 voluntary facial muscles that can express around 20 expressions.[21] For how our eyes filter light so we are not harmed, with the retina having the ability to change its sensitivity to light from ten billion to one.[22] How our ears catch sound waves in the air and end up as electrical signals to our brain.[23] How our vocal chords produce different frequencies with sound waves traveling through our throat, supplying us with our own unique voice.[24] How every part of our body works together for our good.[25] Our bodies are so complex, intricate, detailed, and overwhelmingly amazing, and I know what I have listed is a small part of what they can do. Thank You for creating and breathing life into them.[26] When I went for a walk today, for some reason I stopped to look at my hand and I realized how neat it was... how neat You called me from the dust,[27] and here I am--existing.

Father, thank You also for the creation of the world, nature, and the animals surrounding us.[28] Thank You for the firmament and the lights You put there,[29] for the sun giving us heat and light,[30] how the atmosphere has just the right amount of oxygen, carbon dioxide, and nitrogen for us to live.[31] For the snow and rain making the earth germinate and sprout.[32] Thank You for the dew in the morning which gives water to the ground, plants, bugs, and animals.[33] Thank You for the swallows who place their babies near You.[34]

Thank You for the bees who pollinate our food,[35] and for birds that help bring new tree life through droppings and hiding seeds[36]; for the trees providing anything from oxygen, rest for the animals, food, syrup, shade, firewood, buildings, fences, furniture, décor, toys, paper, boxes, beauty products, instruments, a beautiful sight for our eyes,[37] the cross,[38] and a thousand other things. Thank You for all the food You allow the earth to grow, especially potatoes because they are my favorite. Thank You for the neat things such as how the birds are aware of their migration,[39] can fly all those miles and know exactly where they are going and how to get back. For the detail in a snowflake, and how a water droplet can reflect the world around it, sort of like our lives, and how they reflect what and who we have around us. Thank You for how You clothe the flowers and the grass,[40] for the healing plants and trees,[41] and for the dust of the earth where You formed us from.[42] You are good.

Thank You for filling in any gaps, for being our Father,[43] and Friend.[44] Thank You for family, friends, gifts, abilities, inventions, technology, food, drink, clothes, laughter, and for all the things I do not even know You are doing. Thank You for orchestrating things years in advance which work out perfectly for the moment, for Your wonders planned long ago.[45] Thank You that we all have different works and can help each other,[46] and for giving us everything required for life and godliness.[47] Thank You for providing,[48] protecting,[49] directing my steps,[50] and that my name is "Kristen Michelle Yours".[51]

There are so many things to thank You for Father. I will never be able to thank You for all of them or be able to thank You enough, because all things come from You,[52] and without You none are.[53] Father, thank You.

I love You.

P.S. Father, You are good. Would You like some of my/Your potatoes?

CHAPTER 7

What Place is This?

Mark 6:31 And He said to them, "Come away by yourselves to a secluded place and rest a while." (For there were many *people* coming and going, and they did not even have time to eat.)

Psalm 40:2 He brought me up out of the pit of destruction, out of the miry clay, and He set my feet upon a rock making my footsteps firm.

Psalm 31:19-20 How great is Your goodness, which You have stored up for those who fear You, which You have wrought for those who take refuge in You, before the sons of men! You hide them in the secret place of Your presence from the conspiracies of man; You keep them secretly in a shelter from the strife of tongues.

Psalm 84:10 For a day in Your courts is better than a thousand *outside*. I would rather stand at the threshold of the house of my God than dwell in the tents of wickedness.

Isaiah 41:10 'Do not fear, for I am with you; Do not anxiously look about you, for I am your God. I will strengthen you, surely I will help you, surely I will uphold you with My righteous right hand.'

What Place is This?

Father, Jesus, Holy Spirit,

Thank You.

Father, what place is this, where I am no longer in the valley, but I am not on the mountaintop? It is unfamiliar, sometimes lonely, most of the time silent, but I know I am here because You brought me here instead of death taking me out there. I remember standing in the ashes with everything around me gone and death *still* trying to take me as if the results of the ashes weren't enough. I can see all I came from down there but can't quite see where I am going up there, but I know I need to be here in the in-between for a time. Could it be this place covered by the clouds, and in the safety of the rocks, hidden away, is a place of rest, healing and restoring? I know I need these things but how long will they take? Do I have to stay here long? I will stay as long as You say because I would rather be here with You in an unfamiliar place then try to go somewhere else without You. You say You have a plan for me and a plan for my good.[1] Please help me to believe this as I wait, while I am being bandaged up by You.[2] May I hold Your hand while You complete Your work in me,[3] and may You see through the daze in my face the gratitude I have for all You are doing to help me.

I love You.

P.S. Please, can You hold me in this unfamiliar, lonely, and silent place?

CHAPTER 8

The Plan

Psalm 139:4 Even before there is a word on my tongue, behold, O LORD, You know it all.

Genesis 1:21 God created the great sea monsters and every living creature that moves, with which the waters swarmed after their kind, and every winged bird after its kind; and God saw that it was good.

Psalm 39:7 "And now, Lord, for what do I wait? My hope is in You.

Psalm 31:9 Be gracious to me, O LORD, for I am in distress; my eye is wasted away from grief, my soul and my body *also*.

Proverbs 3:5-6 Trust in the LORD with all your heart and do not lean on your own understanding. In all your ways acknowledge Him, and He will make your paths straight.

The Plan

Father, Jesus, Holy Spirit,

Thank You.

Father, as I drove home from work tonight and watched the headlights reflect off the snow falling, my heart started to worry about the birds outside. I know You heard my heart before I said the words, "What about the birds?", with a posture of fear on how the snow and cold is affecting them. You answered me right away. Sometimes when You speak there is so much to what You say and so much in just a short moment. So sometimes it is hard to capture everything You say with human words, but tonight You said something like, You made the birds knowing what conditions could happen, and You are taking care of them. I then remembered how the feathers of these birds work, and how their feathers work for their good in lots of ways, and one of the ways is so they can regulate their body temperatures and trap warm air next to their bodies.[1] You also made some of these birds with abilities to adapt to the cold with their blood temperature dropping at night[2] or the ability for them to activate muscles to contract, kind of like shivering, to keep them warm.[3] Why do I sometimes forget You made the earth and all that is in it?[4] You knew these conditions would come and made the birds accordingly.

After my heart rested from the worry, I started to wonder, as I drove home from work once again, if this was still part of the plan. For me being here in this town, working at this place, and me not being where I want to be yet--is it still part of the plan? Day in and day out, is this the plan? Because I am so sad and have been trying to hang on. I am so discouraged. You say hope delayed makes the heart sick[5]; my heart is so sick. Father, I am so thankful for what You have done and for all You have brought me through. I am just being honest with You that I feel like I am barely holding on as I try to wait.

Some days when I pull in my driveway, I do not have the strength to get out of the car. I just sit there and wonder if this is it, and how I cannot seem to get to where I want to be. Did You make me knowing these conditions would come for me where I am sad, uncertain of the plan, and am barely holding on?

I do not know what to do anymore or what to pray anymore. I have been asking for help and for things to change for a while now. I have written You letters, I have screamed out Your name, I have prayed, I have worshiped, I have fasted.[6] I have prayed everything I can think and have asked the Holy Spirit what to pray for, too.[7] Along with wondering if this is still part of the plan for me, I am now wondering if there are enough bottles for my tears[8] that are filled with messages of sadness and pain.

Father I do not know what I am doing or what is going on. Is there something I am missing? Are You trying to show me something?

Please help me each day as I drive home and sit in the driveway to know You made me accordingly too, where I can make it through these conditions that have come. Perhaps this is the plan; perhaps the plan all along was for me to learn to trust in You. Please could You provide a plant to ease the discomfort like You did for Jonah,[9] as I wait for You.

I love You.

P.S. Thank You for the over one hundred animals I get to see on the way to work each day. The sheep and donkeys are my favorite, but You already knew they would be when You placed me in this town, in this house, on this path, to help me smile as I wait for You expectantly.

CHAPTER 9

Where Are You?

Isaiah 38:14 (CSB) I chirp like a swallow or a crane; I moan like a dove. My eyes grow weak looking upward. Lord, I am oppressed; support me.

Psalm 38:21 Do not forsake me, O LORD; O my God, do not be far from me!

Deuteronomy 32:11 "Like an eagle that stirs up its nest, that hovers over its young, He spread His wings and caught them, He carried them on His pinions.

Job 36:7 "He does not withdraw His eyes from the righteous; but with kings on the throne He has seated them forever, and they are exalted.

Mark 9:24 Immediately the boy's father cried out and said, "I do believe; help my unbelief."

Where Are You

Father, Jesus, Holy Spirit,

Thank You.

Father, suddenly I feel as if You have left; as if I was sitting in a nest with You and then You flew away. Where are You? I am just sitting up here with big eyes looking around for You. Are You upset with me? Did You fly to another tree? Is Your gaze still[1] on me and I just cannot see You? How come I feel this way? Why can I not see You, feel You, or smell You? Would You at least breathe on me so I know You are near? Help me believe every letter of every word You speak, that You are near[2] and You will not leave me[3]; help my unbelief.[4]

. . . .

I am sorry I yelled at You… it just doesn't feel well with my soul.[5] Father, here I am; I am right here; where are You?

I love You.

P.S. Am I in the shadow of Your wings[6] and this is the reason I cannot see You?

CHAPTER 10
7th Day

Psalm 116:8 For You have rescued my soul from death, my eyes from tears, my feet from stumbling.

Joshua 6:1-4 Now Jericho was tightly shut because of the sons of Israel; no one went out and no one came in. The LORD said to Joshua, "See, I have given Jericho into your hand, with its king *and* the valiant warriors. You shall march around the city, all the men of war circling the city once. You shall do so for six days. Also, seven priests shall carry seven trumpets of rams' horns before the ark; then on the seventh day you shall march around the city seven times, and the priests shall blow the trumpets.

Joshua 6:10 But Joshua commanded the people, saying, "You shall not shout nor let your voice be heard nor let a word proceed out of your mouth, until the day I tell you, 'Shout!' Then you shall shout!"

Psalm 27:14 Wait for the LORD; be strong and let your heart take courage; yes, wait for the LORD.

Luke 11:2 (CSB) He said to them, "Whenever you pray, say, Father, your name be honored as holy. Your kingdom come.

7th Day

Father, Jesus, Holy Spirit,

Thank You.

Father, thank You for all the things You just brought me through, saved me from, and worked out for me. I know I am now at the wall[1] to a new season and I had to go on a journey first to get to the wall. That journey was a long season of tears, and it was awful. I hope I never have to experience a season like that again. I have been in the in-between for a while now, but I am ready for the mountain. I have been circling and circling and am now ready to shout. Please--from Your Tower that protects me[2] and can see all things, please let me know when it is time to shout so I can advance. Things have been harder lately for me, and I am wondering if it is because it is the 7th day, and I have been circling more than one lap.[3] What lap am I on? I do not want to shout before it is time, but only when it is Your will and Your time. Until I hear the new season has been handed over to me, I will keep circling.

I honor Your name as Holy.[4]

I love You.

P.S. Please could You send an army of angels to help me circle the wall so there can be a breakthrough.

CHAPTER 11

My Heart is Past Sick

Psalm 143:4 Therefore my spirit is overwhelmed within me; my heart is appalled within me.

Jeremiah 8:18 My sorrow is beyond healing, my heart is faint *within me!*

Proverbs 13:12 Hope deferred makes the heart sick, but desire fulfilled is a tree of life.

Jonah 2:5 (CSB) The water engulfed me up to the neck; the watery depths overcame me; seaweed was wrapped around my head.

Job 34:12-13 "Surely, God will not act wickedly, and the Almighty will not pervert justice. "Who gave Him authority over the earth? And who has laid *on Him* the whole world?

My Heart is Past Sick

Father, Jesus, Holy Spirit,

Thank You.

Months have gone by since I thought I was at the wall[1]; on day seven, wondering what lap I was on. I was holding on to the hope I had left, believing a breakthrough was finally coming. I have not heard any mention that it is time to shout,[2] and I feel more alone each round I go. Am I at the right wall? I do not know if I have it in me to keep going. I can barely stand, my bow is bent, scratched, and hardly together; the tears never end. Now after years of fighting, hoping, and believing, suddenly everything is crumbling around me. I keep telling myself everything is okay, and You are taking care of it, but it is getting hard to breathe. I do not understand, why would it get worse? Why are You letting this happen to me? I read Your words every day; I talk to You all day every day; I try my best to do everything You say. I fight the enemy with my bow, but I am stunned, bullied, attacked, harassed[3] by him time and time again. Is the enemy laughing at me when I scream out in anguish? Or when I sit and shake, is he looking at me hoping today is the day my heart gives way?

I stare out the door waiting expectantly for You, but now I just want to go lie down because it seems as if You are not going to move. What is going on? Why are You not sending help? I have asked and asked. How is this for my good[4] when I cry, shake, and scream? I know Your thoughts and ways are not mine,[5] but my feelings and tears *are*. I am supposed to tell You all my cares because You care about me,[6] but it is hard to feel like someone cares when they do not respond or speak. This is where people like to say someone needs to have faith. If I didn't have faith, then I wouldn't be writing this letter to You--especially after all these years of fighting. Faith is not the absence of feelings and questions. Faith is knowing where my help comes from and looking to You for it, petitioning to You.[7] Faith is the reality of my hope,[8] and I know my only hope is You.

I am in a giant mess and feel as if I have been kidding myself that a better future is ahead. That my hope seeds would produce something. My heart is past sick.[9] Please tell me there is some epic reason I am being buried in rubble.

Please tell me the pieces of rubble I am standing in are pieces of the wall that finally fell down. Please, Father, please.

Jesus, You said in Matthew 26:53 "Or do you think that I cannot call on my Father, and he will provide me here and now with more than twelve legions of angels?" Would it be okay if I ask Him for angels to come help me? For them to be sent in every area of my life and break all hindrances, to break what is keeping good things from me, to get rid of anything not of You? You say You will fly on the wings of the wind and rescue,[10] please, please will You? Please thunder from Heaven and speak.[11] Please unwrap the seaweed from around my head.[12] Please personally restore and redeem.[13] Please provide abundantly.[14] Please could my hope seeds begin to germinate and not stay in a state of dormancy. Since faith is the reality of what is hoped for, then please could all I have faith for be reality? I do not deserve it, but I ask for it anyway.

I know we all think our stories are like Job's at some point in our life. Are You showing the enemy I choose You, or is there something left that You are trying to correct in me? Please help me to not justify myself, like Elihu talks about.[15] Please show me what I need to do.

You are the Creator of all things,[16] and no one put You in charge.[17] I was not there when You established the earth.[18] You do no wrong and do not pervert justice.[19] You do not have to speak or speak to me.[20] I repent and I am sorry, because You are good and Your ways are just,[21] forever and always.

Thank You.

P.S. I still love You.

CHAPTER 12

Claiming a Dependent

Ephesians 2:18-20 for through Him we both have our access in one Spirit to the Father. So then you are no longer strangers and aliens, but you are fellow citizens with the saints, and are of God's household, having been built on the foundation of the apostles and prophets, Christ Jesus Himself being the corner *stone,*

Matthew 6:30-33 But if God so clothes the grass of the field, which is *alive* today and tomorrow is thrown into the furnace, *will He* not much more *clothe* you? You of little faith! Do not worry then, saying, 'What will we eat?' or 'What will we drink?' or 'What will we wear for clothing?' For the Gentiles eagerly seek all these things; for your heavenly Father knows that you need all these things. But seek first His kingdom and His righteousness, and all these things will be added to you.

Psalm 51:2 Wash me thoroughly from my iniquity and cleanse me from my sin.

John 14:6 Jesus said to him, "I am the way, and the truth, and the life; no one comes to the Father but through Me.

Ephesians 1:13-14 In Him, you also, after listening to the message of truth, the gospel of your salvation--having also believed, you were sealed in Him with the Holy Spirit of promise, who is given as a pledge of our inheritance, with a view to the redemption of *God's own* possession, to the praise of His glory.

Claiming a Dependent

Father, Jesus, Holy Spirit,

Thank You.

Father, You have claimed me in Your household.[1] I am completely dependent on You.[2] I cannot do anything without You. Thank You for Your provisions and for feeding me.[3] Thank You for washing me clean.[4] For teaching me the Way,[5] for protecting me,[6] for taking care of me when I am sick,[7] for all the bandages on my knees,[8] for allowing me to sleep each night,[9] and for providing the down payment for what is ahead.[10] I cannot be independent of You.[11] I need Thee.[12]

I love You.

P.S. Jesus, thank You for my retirement plan. I know I will be secure. I look forward to retiring from this earth and seeing the place You have prepared for me.[13]

CHAPTER 13

My Purpose

Psalm 144:4 Man is like a mere breath; his days are like a passing shadow.

Philippians 2:3 Do nothing from selfishness or empty conceit, but with humility of mind regard one another as more important than yourselves;

Isaiah 43:6-7 "I will say to the north, 'Give *them* up!' And to the south, 'Do not hold *them* back.' Bring My sons from afar and My daughters from the ends of the earth, everyone who is called by My name, and whom I have created for My glory, whom I have formed, even whom I have made."

Ephesians 2:10 For we are His workmanship, created in Christ Jesus for good works, which God prepared beforehand so that we would walk in them.

2 Peter 1:3 seeing that His divine power has granted to us everything pertaining to life and godliness, through the true knowledge of Him who called us by His own glory and excellence.

My Purpose

Father, Jesus, Holy Spirit,

Thank You.

Father, I decided I would go and check on my unfortunate favorite organization today, to see what they were doing and all the progress they are making. I know I have to warn myself before I look, because the work they do is tough and tough to see. Knowing this I went and looked to see what they had been doing and, once again, my heart just broke to see the things I did. Father I know this life is but a breath,[1] but why do we make is so hard for everyone to breathe? We are creating needs for one another instead of loving one another. I desire so much for all mankind to look to You, for us to love You, take hold of all the fruit of the Spirit,[2] and have compassion on all Your creation, like You do.[3]

Father, there is so much suffering in the world, the aftereffects of sin, and it is unfathomable. Sometimes I feel as if there is no point with me trying to help because there is so much wrong. I do not feel like I could ever make a dent in the suffering. But you kindly reminded me You didn't give up because there was so much wrong, but You would rescue even if there was only one,[4] to stop the suffering for one. Thank You for reminding me that each and every life in all creation means something to You.

Father, I know my purpose is to be loved by You,[5] worship You,[6] and do whatever You say including the good works You have prepared for me to do.[7] Thank You for reminding me You have designed,[8] gifted,[9] and given me all I need,[10] to do whatever You say.

Thank You for loving me. Thank You for choosing me.[11] I choose You. Father, may I summon my courage like Jehoiada did,[12] to do the work You have prepared for me to do.

I worship You forever. I love You.

P.S. Holy Spirit, the puppy barking outside right now, is he okay? It is really late for him to be barking like this. Maybe he is cold. Could You send an angel to be with him?

CHAPTER 14

Music

Psalm 148:7-13 Praise the LORD from the earth, sea monsters and all deeps; fire and hail, snow and clouds; stormy wind, fulfilling His word; mountains and all hills; fruit trees and all cedars; beasts and all cattle; creeping things and winged fowl; kings of the earth and all peoples; princes and all judges of the earth; both young men and virgins; old men and children. Let them praise the name of the LORD, for His name alone is exalted; His glory is above earth and heaven.

Psalm 104:12 Beside them the birds of the heavens dwell; they lift up *their* voices among the branches.

1 Chronicles 13:8 David and all Israel were celebrating before God with all *their* might, even with songs and with lyres, harps, tambourines, cymbals and with trumpets.

Ezekiel 36:26 Moreover, I will give you a new heart and put a new spirit within you; and I will remove the heart of stone from your flesh and give you a heart of flesh.

Psalm 40:3 He put a new song in my mouth, a song of praise to our God; many will see and fear and will trust in the LORD.

Music

Father, Jesus, Holy Spirit,

Thank You.

Father, it amazes me when I think about Your creation. How it makes its sound to honor You. Every leap of the sea, flap of the air, trot of the field, creep on the ground, and rustle of the forest. Every rush of water, whirl of wind, drop of hail, and rumble of thunder.[1] Even how when the wind blows, the trees rock and the leaves roll, and how there are over ten thousand species of birds (that we humans know of)[2] who have their own unique beautiful notes they sing to You. It is like Your song (creation) is always playing, a song which began with a frequency, the frequency of Your voice.[3] Didn't John describe Your voice like a trumpet?[4]

If all of this is going on in creation, why do Your people argue about the sounds, the genre, style or volume of music we as humans make, listen to, and worship You with? They especially argue about the sounds of a worship setting, how loud, what kind of instruments and what it should sound like. Which doesn't make sense because the worship is about You. Just because a song has a pleasing sound to someone doesn't mean anything. It could have words of defeat all through it, no matter how loud it is. Then a song that is not someone's preferred style may be a song with words of life all through it.

There are many references in Your Word of music, songs, and instruments. In the Old Testament there are so many times when people were making music for You, especially in David's time. With lyres, harps, tambourines, strings, flutes, trumpets, sounds of horns, and crashing of cymbals.[5] Didn't David and all of Israel dance in front of You with all their might with songs and some of these same instruments?[6] Didn't Hezekiah and his people turn up the music and praise You?[7] We see mention of music in the New Testament too, especially about singing songs to You. How Paul and Silas were singing.[8] Or in the Parable of the Lost Son, didn't the older son hear music and dancing?[9] Or didn't John say the four living creatures and the twenty-four elders had a harp and sang a new song?[10] How does anyone know what the genre, style, or volume of any of this was?

Maybe genre, style, or volume is not what we should focus on. No matter what our ears hear, or where in the world or in Heaven it comes from, or how different it sounds, if it is made for You and truly points to the same One—You—isn't that what matters? Shouldn't we want this? How can anyone have anything to argue about if people are turning to You? Isn't the true genre a matter of the heart anyway? What if all You hear is the heart? Isn't it where the most beautiful sound can be found, the song You put there? The song which changes the style of our hearts[11] and gives us the desire to use all of our life, gifts, and abilities for You? The song that originally sounded like we are awesome but now sounds like You are awesome? The song that can be so loud, yet it has no volume? The song that when You hear all of our hearts singing together, sounds like a multitude of praise?[12]

Father, my song to You does not change, no matter what sounds I hear, utter, or play. You are worthy.[13]

I love You.

P.S. This is my story, and this is my song.[14]

CHAPTER 15

The Grass

Malachi 2:10 "Do we not all have one father? Has not one God created us? Why do we deal treacherously each against his brother so as to profane the covenant of our fathers?

Isaiah 40:5-7 Then the glory of the LORD will be revealed, and all flesh will see *it* together; for the mouth of the LORD has spoken." A voice says, "Call out." Then he answered, "What shall I call out?" All flesh is grass, and all its loveliness is like the flower of the field. The grass withers, the flower fades, when the breath of the LORD blows upon it; surely the people are grass.

Psalm 14:2 (CSB) The Lord looks down from heaven on the human race to see if there is one who is wise, one who seeks God.

John 6:63 It is the Spirit who gives life; the flesh profits nothing; the words that I have spoken to you are spirit and are life.

Jeremiah 17:7-8 "Blessed is the man who trusts in the LORD and whose trust is the LORD. "For he will be like a tree planted by the water, that extends its roots by a stream and will not fear when the heat comes; but its leaves will be green, and it will not be anxious in a year of drought nor cease to yield fruit.

The Grass

Father, Jesus, Holy Spirit,

Thank You.

Father, I am always in awe of Your creation. How beautiful it is and how it all points to You. How the trees, flowers, and even grass all point to You. How it is all for Your glory and for our good.[1] I have been thinking a lot lately about the grass and how I wish everyone could see it. A lot of times Your creation is a great representation of our lives, and I believe the grass is a perfect one.

I have been thinking lately how there are all kinds of grass, some tall, short, thick, thin, light, dark, and every shade in-between. Some grass has texture, wrinkles, and some is smooth. When it comes down to it, even though there are some differences in appearance, it is all still green, and all still grass, and all still comes from the same One: You.[2]

Is it a coincidence I would be reading through Isaiah right now and thinking about the grass? How neat is Your timing, because You say all humanity is grass.[3] Could it be we are all grass, all the same color but varying shades, all the same race, the human race,[4] and all breathing Your breath by Your grace?[5] (Thank You for showing me something neat in a Word document-- when I go to more colors, then custom colors, and click on any color, to the right are all the shades of the same color).

Father if we are grass where our outer fades away, but our inner remains,[6] wouldn't this be what matters? When I was walking the other day, I looked down and saw some grass that was brown. You showed me there is either dead grass or grass that has been given life through You.[7] Just like grass, we need the Water and the Light to be brought to life.[8] The only divide is whether our souls are dead or alive. Even for us who are alive there is no Jew or Gentile, we are all one in Jesus.[9] The war is not against our flesh but between good and evil, Heaven and Hell.[10] Please help us to not be tricked by the enemy.

We are all just grass, and if we are with You, the Father of Truth,[11] then we are beautifully made alive through You.

Thank You.

I love You.

P.S. Father, please help us to not look on the outer appearance but see the inner person like You do.[12] I pray for a movement against evil and a movement towards You, so the world can be greener.

CHAPTER 16

The Guilty

Isaiah 53:5-6 But He was pierced through for our transgressions, He was crushed for our iniquities; the chastening for our well-being *fell* upon Him, and by His scourging we are healed. All of us like sheep have gone astray, each of us has turned to his own way; but the LORD has caused the iniquity of us all to fall on Him.

Proverbs 24:17-18 Do not rejoice when your enemy falls, and do not let your heart be glad when he stumbles; or the LORD will see *it* and be displeased, and turn His anger away from him.

Luke 6:27-28 "But I say to you who hear, love your enemies, do good to those who hate you, bless those who curse you, pray for those who mistreat you.

Titus 3:3-7 For we also once were foolish ourselves, disobedient, deceived, enslaved to various lusts and pleasures, spending our life in malice and envy, hateful, hating one another. But when the kindness of God our Savior and *His* love for mankind appeared, He saved us, not on the basis of deeds which we have done in righteousness, but according to His mercy, by the washing of regeneration and renewing by the Holy Spirit, whom He poured out upon us richly through Jesus Christ our Savior, so that being justified by His grace we would be made heirs according to *the* hope of eternal life.

Matthew 27:37 And above His head they put up the charge against Him which read, "THIS IS JESUS THE KING OF THE JEWS."

The Guilty

Father, Jesus, Holy Spirit,

Thank You.

Jesus, please could You help me see what You see in all Your creation,[1] because Your breath is inside all those who are breathing.[2] You fearfully and wonderfully[3] made all whose hearts beat. Jesus show me how to love the innocent AND the guilty, because I was guilty once too.[4] Even though You were crushed because of me and my sins took Your breath away,[5] You showed me love, kindness, and compassion--none of which I deserved, still don't, and never will. Yet while I was bad, You still loved me.[6] While I was Your enemy, You gave Your life to save me.[7] Show me how to love with my whole heart not partially.[8] Please give me strength and show me how to pray for both the innocent and the guilty and for both of their families.

You are the God of peace,[9] love,[10] the Bright Morning Star,[11] with scars from nails I put in Your hands. Show me how to love like You, which enables me to look past my hurt and respond with the same grace,[12] while I remember again that I was once the guilty one, too. Thank You for not throwing me away, for not hating me in Your heart, or secretly wishing ill towards me,[13] but yet saving me.[14] Please let me kiss Your scars and catch Your tears as I remember the grace You gave me when You didn't have to.

I love You Jesus. You are the best forever!

P.S. You truly *are* the King and the King of the Jews.[15]

CHAPTER 17

The Fight

Psalm 34:7 The angel of the LORD encamps around those who fear Him, and rescues them.

2 Timothy 1:7 For God has not given us a spirit of timidity, but of power and love and discipline.

Proverbs 28:1 The wicked flee when no one is pursuing, but the righteous are bold as a lion.

Psalm 91:5 You will not be afraid of the terror by night, or of the arrow that flies by day;

2 Chronicles 32:8 With him is *only* an arm of flesh, but with us is the LORD our God to help us and to fight our battles." And the people relied on the words of Hezekiah king of Judah.

The Fight

Father, Jesus, Holy Spirit,

Thank You.

Father, one of my friends is struggling and has been for a long time. I know You know, and You know everything that is the root of the struggle. Sometimes things happen to us, things which are not fair, or we never asked for. Sometimes things happen because we do them, not understanding what we are doing. Sometimes things happen because the enemy is simply out to get us in any and every way he can. He knows exactly where, what, and how to tell us things we will believe.[1]

We know Your Word says there will be trouble here and to have courage, because You have overcome the trouble of the here and now.[2] Sometimes, Father, in the midst of the fight that seems relentless, it is hard to keep courage. In the midst of the lies of defeat told in a way only we would believe, it is hard sometimes to remember the word defeat isn't even in our "dictionary", except where it says Jesus defeated the enemy.[3]

Father, I ask again that You could please break whatever is breaking my friend. Please, could You send angels out into all the areas involved in what is going on to fight any force not of You. I confess Psalm 91 over their life. Holy Spirit, please could You reach up and touch my friend's heart right here in this moment and calm it. Please breathe throughout the room they are in right now. Please help them to discern Your truth as You breathe for them and help them to not listen to any of the babble of the enemy. Jesus, please, could You hold them and show them whatever it is they need to see.

Father, I ask that, after they are comforted, they can remember that they have a Spirit of power[4]; for them to be able to raise their head up even if the tears are still falling down; to be bold as a lion because You made them righteous.[5] I ask that perhaps they no longer just watch as all the arrows fly by[6] but, with the Power within them, they could catch those arrows and throw them back at the enemy. Father, please, could my friend's cries for help reach Your ears?[7] Please, fly on the wings of the wind[8] and rescue my friend from the enemy. Please, could You shoot Your arrows[9] and blow out Your fire on the enemy[10] and destroy him, the one hurting my friend?

Father, please give all of us who surround my friend the wisdom[11] and the words to know how to help. Holy Spirit, please intercede and also help us know what to pray for.[12] Father, I will stand with my friend and throw the arrows back at the enemy too, even when they start to lose hope.

I thank You for them, Father. Thank You for their breath. Thank You for allowing me to know them and for all the times they have thrown the arrows for me when I have lost hope. Father may this fight be over. May we all not rest on the lies of the enemy when we get weary and tired because we are not the ones in the ring: You are.

I love You.

P.S. Father, may the new season arrive for my friend and the flowers start to bloom once again. Thank You.

CHAPTER 18

The Course

2 Timothy 2:23-26 But refuse foolish and ignorant speculations, knowing that they produce quarrels. The Lord's bond-servant must not be quarrelsome, but be kind to all, able to teach, patient when wronged, with gentleness correcting those who are in opposition, if perhaps God may grant them repentance leading to the knowledge of the truth, and they may come to their senses *and escape* from the snare of the devil, having been held captive by him to do his will.

Romans 12:14-19 Bless those who persecute you; bless and do not curse. Rejoice with those who rejoice, and weep with those who weep. Be of the same mind toward one another; do not be haughty in mind, but associate with the lowly. Do not be wise in your own estimation. Never pay back evil for evil to anyone. Respect what is right in the sight of all men. If possible, so far as it depends on you, be at peace with all men. Never take your own revenge, beloved, but leave room for the wrath *of God,* for it is written, "VENGEANCE IS MINE, I WILL REPAY," says the Lord.

Matthew 12:30 He who is not with Me is against Me; and he who does not gather with Me scatters.

Exodus 34:14 (CSB) Because the Lord is jealous for his reputation, you are never to bow down to another god. He is a jealous God.

Psalm 103:2-5 Bless the LORD, O my soul, and forget none of His benefits; who pardons all your iniquities, who heals all your diseases; who redeems your life from the pit, who crowns you with lovingkindness and compassion; who satisfies your years with good things, *so that* your youth is renewed like the eagle.

The Course

Father, Jesus, Holy Spirit,

Thank You.

Father, I know my spirit isn't the only one that is sad with everything going on in this first world and is longing for the second world; with all the deceit and all of the enemy's tricks. How people are responding, treating each other, and talking about others, even us who follow You. The waters are big, and the wind is strong right now. Help us to not focus on the wind and the waves, but to keep our eyes only on You.

The enemy, disguising himself as an angel of light[1] (which he is not because You tell us that he was a murderer from the beginning and is a liar[2]), is doing the same things he has always been doing. Since he disguises himself as light, sometimes things may seem like they are good but are just one of his schemes[3] to try and trick us--all to his delight. We have no idea how intricately woven his work is, the secret things of him.[4] He is also trying to divide us, those of us who are truly Yours, who confess with our mouths that You, Jesus Christ, are Lord and believe God raised You from the dead.[5] Help us to not let him divide us or be discouraged with the flaming arrows[6] he is throwing at us. Help us to not throw arrows at each other, because we are all the same body.[7] Please help us to not allow him to push us off the path, where we end up rolling around in the thorn bushes.

Could it be the enemy can only trick and divide us, when we use our own definitions and opinions, not looking through the lens of You? Your Word says to have like minds[8] and to live in harmony with one another.[9] We are all imperfect and all of our imperfections look different; this is why we need You. The secret is You. The answer is You. You are the remedy, the cure, the solution.

Help us all to remember part of keeping our eyes on You is keeping our eyes on Your words; to remember Your thoughts are higher and ways are higher.[10] Help us to see things through Your perspective. Please help us to not be a stumbling block[11] but be weapons for righteousness[12] no matter what happens.

Help us to understand how to do what Your Word says. To take the lead in showing honor,[13] to do what is honorable in everyone's eyes[14] and, if possible, to live at peace with everyone.[15] To not quarrel but be gentle and patient, instructing our opponents with gentleness.[16] To do good to those who hate us,[17] bless those who curse us and pray for those who treat us wrong,[18] and if our enemies are hungry or thirsty to feed them and give them something to drink.[19] To not hold a grudge against anyone in our community.[20] To gather and not scatter.[21] To pray for everyone; kings, those in authority,[22] our enemies,[23] and intercede for the saints.[24] To not be conformed to this world,[25] to not participate in the works of darkness.[26] To seek You[27] and write Your words on our hearts.[28] To have no other gods[29] and only bow to You.[30] Help us to remember the greatest and most important command is to love You with all our heart, soul and mind; and that the second one is to love our neighbor as ourself.[31]

No matter what happens, please help us to get to the truth of what really matters: You. Please help us to ask You for wisdom and discernment so we can understand and not be tricked. Even though many times it may not seem like it to this world, that those who follow You Jesus, have it the best, please help us remember we are the privileged ones, not forgetting all of Your benefits.[32] We are beneficiaries of Your love, power, and grace. There is no one more privileged than those whose hand is being held by You, the One who can take the spirit and breath away from everything,[33] we are Your treasured ones.[34]

This world may never know how many licks it takes to get to the center of a Tootsie Pop, but it will know, Jesus, that You are Lord and King. For those of us who already know and follow You, please help us to not give in, give up, or give way. Please help us to hold on,[35] to hold on to Truth[36] and to steady the course to You because in the end righteousness will win.[37]

I love You.

P.S. Please could You send angels to cover those animals who cannot get away from the flood waters, fire, and smoke? Thank You.

CHAPTER 19

Questions

Genesis 2:19 Out of the ground the LORD God formed every beast of the field and every bird of the sky, and brought *them* to the man to see what he would call them; and whatever the man called a living creature, that was its name.

1 Corinthians 12:4-6 Now there are varieties of gifts, but the same Spirit. And there are varieties of ministries, and the same Lord. There are varieties of effects, but the same God who works all things in all *persons*.

Ezekiel 1:28 As the appearance of the rainbow in the clouds on a rainy day, so *was* the appearance of the surrounding radiance. Such *was* the appearance of the likeness of the glory of the LORD. And when I saw *it*, I fell on my face and heard a voice speaking.

Revelation 8:1 When the Lamb broke the seventh seal, there was silence in heaven for about half an hour.

Revelation 19:11 And I saw heaven opened, and behold, a white horse, and He who sat on it *is* called Faithful and True, and in righteousness He judges and wages war.

Questions

Father, Jesus, Holy Spirit,

Thank You.

When You had me in mind to call me forth from the ground,[1] You knew I would be a wonderer. My mind is constantly full of wonder, whether with things I read in Your Word or things in this life. Until I get to Where I am going, here are a few of the millions of wonders in my mind. I know I do not need to know any of the answers, because all I need to know is: You Are.

1. What did You do before You created the heavens and the earth? Was there a *before*, before the beginning?

2. When You talk about two of every creature that has the breath of life entering the ark,[2] was there water on the boat for the creatures like beavers, semi-aquatic turtles, or penguins? Did Noah have the ability to keep different temperatures on the boat?

3. When You say to preach the gospel to all creation,[3] does this mean to show love (because You are love),[4] to everything You created such as the animals?

4. If I pray now for something that happened in the past before I was born, did You hear it back then? When I hug You in my thoughts, do You feel it?

5. Father, why do we as humans have such weird sayings, some spoken with references to death such as the saying, "kill two birds with one stone", when we are talking about accomplishing two things with one effort? Why can't we speak life and say something like "feed two birds with one seed"? Jesus, You fed the crowds of 4,000[5] and 5,000,[6] so why couldn't we say, "feed two birds with one seed"?

6. How old was Adam when You made him? How much time went by before he met Eve?

7. Father, we have this question we ask sometimes: if the chicken or the egg came first. Would the answer be chicken because You said

You made the animals according to their kind[7] and then Adam named them?[8] Or was it, You made an egg, then it hatched and then Adam named it?

8. The man in the Amazon who is all alone, is he lonely? Could he have a friend? How do You talk to him? I bet it is neat how You reveal Yourself to him. Are there more people like this in the world that we do not know of?

9. Is it okay to use creative lighting in worship settings? It seems as if You like creative lighting because of the lights You created: lightning, heat lightning, stars, aurora lights, halos, sun dogs, red sprits, rainbows, even the neat lightning bugs and sea sparkles. Oh, and the sun, the green flash, and the moon. Your Word says You are Light[9]. It even talks about lightning coming from Your throne,[10] and rays flashing from Your hand.[11]

10. Whenever I hear the phrase "full time ministry," it is always associated with a position in a church organization. Wouldn't full time ministry be for anyone who is employed by You? Shouldn't we all be gathering people to You? Isn't the mission the same whether we work for a church organization or outside of one? To go into all the world[12] telling them to be reconciled to You?[13] You also say there are different ministries,[14] so would there be just one that is full-time? Is this similar to how there are different branches of the military, all having different works but the same mission? Wouldn't it be the same for us who are employed by You, to work full-time gathering people to You no matter where we go or what we do?

11. When I was little, why did I think that maybe the enemy just needed a friend, and he wouldn't be so mean? This is not true at all; he is mean all the time; and all the time he is mean, no matter what.

12. If I have authority over the animals[15] (to look after and care for), could this be another reminder the serpent/Satan has no authority over me?[16]

13. Do You know all the bugs individually and can tell them apart? It is weird to think how they have tiny hearts.[17]

14. Jesus what did You look like before You came to the earth? Did You decide what You would look like when You came here and what foods and smells You would like?

15. Jesus when You were a baby, how did Your mind work since You are God?[18] Was Your mind fully aware? When the Wise Men came to You,[19] did You know it at the time? When You would play with Your friends as You grew up, was it hard knowing their futures, if in their futures, they never accepted You?

16. Jesus, when those people wanted to stone the woman who committed adultery, what were You writing on the ground?[20]

17. Jesus, when you came to the region of the Gerasenes and sent the demons in the pigs and they went over the cliff,[21] did the demons perish with the pigs?

18. Those people who came out of the tombs after Your resurrection,[22] Jesus, did they die again?

19. I was wondering if You have a favorite animal. Is it the Lamb?[23] Or maybe the Dove?[24]

20. What is Your favorite thing to appear as? Is it hope?[25]

21. What is Your favorite color? Is it light? Is it light because to get visible light that humans see, it takes all the colors combined in the visible spectrum? Is this also why You are described as having rainbow colors[26]--because You are Light?[27]

22. I always thought there was no time after this life. When John said there was silence in Heaven for about half an hour[28] and the tree of life will bear fruit every month,[29] does this mean there is time?

23. When John says the sea will no longer exist after this earth,[30] is this the literal sea? If so, will there be something better, or will we need the space for all the people who will be there? Will the new earth be bigger or have different mountains in different places? Will there still be seasons? Your Word says You will be our Light and not the sun[31]; will there be a set temperature? The twelve fruits from the tree of life, what kind of fruits are these?[32]

24. In our current world, is it getting hotter or colder? It seems like it is getting colder since the world keeps moving further and further away from You—the Son[33]. This will always change the climate. It rained a whole lot that one time.[34]

25. The trumpets being blown in Revelation[35]--can we hear them or just see the events that happen after they are blown?

26. Jesus, the horse You will be riding when You come back to the earth,[36] is he a spirit horse or a flesh horse? If he is flesh, where is he? Is he with You now or has he not been born yet?

27. Do all angels fly? When You say we will be like the angels at the resurrection, not marrying or given in marriage,[37] will we be like the angels in other ways? Might I be able to fly, too?

28. Will we continue to be like the angels at the resurrection, when all things are restored[38] and there is a new earth?[39] I was wondering since Adam and Eve were married[40] before sin and the fall; will this be a part of what is restored and new?

29. The babies who were never born on this earth, will they be born on the new earth? Will all the extinct animals be there on the new earth? Will we be friends with the angels?

30. If all Your people bought an extra Bible and gave it away to someone, or placed it in a place for someone to come across, would this make a big impact? Since Your Word is a sword,[41] would this be another way for us to fight for the Kingdom, by placing more of Your Weapon around the world?

I love You.

P.S. Since all my days are written in Your book,[42] are all the questions I am ever going to ask written in there too?

FRIENDS

CHAPTER 20

Comparison

2 Corinthians 6:18 "And I will be a father to you, and you shall be sons and daughters to Me," says the Lord Almighty.

Proverbs 29:25 The fear of man brings a snare, but he who trusts in the LORD will be exalted.

Matthew 7:11 If you then, being evil, know how to give good gifts to your children, how much more will your Father who is in heaven give what is good to those who ask Him!

Isaiah 40:22 (CSB) God is enthroned above the circle of the earth; its inhabitants are like grasshoppers. He stretches out the heavens like thin cloth and spreads them out like a tent to live in.

1 John 5:3-5 (CSB) For this is what love for God is: to keep his commands. And his commands are not a burden, because everyone who has been born of God conquers the world. This is the victory that has conquered the world: our faith. Who is the one who conquers the world but the one who believes that Jesus is the Son of God?

Comparison

Hi Friend,

Sometimes when we talk, I see there is something bothering you a lot and it makes me so sad. This something is the same thing that many of us struggle with, including me.

The *something* is comparison. I think the act of comparison is when we try to prove to ourselves that we are valuable, special, and worth what others are worth. Many times when we compare, in our minds we think we fall short. We think we do not have enough, such as enough money, possessions, or friends. Or that we haven't been given enough with our abilities, skills, and opportunities. We think the reason we do not have these things is because we alone are not enough. We tell ourselves all kinds of horrible lies. It is nonsense, really, what we do to ourselves.

Sometimes you and I both allow others to tell us the value of our being. People still have the ability to dictate our worth in terms of what we think in our minds. I have heard this a lot lately; and then I hear you try to convince yourself that you are good enough and valuable. I catch myself doing the same things. But here is the thing: we have to get to a place where we tell ourselves and start to believe that the King already spoke concerning this, and nothing can change it.

You already are the King's daughter.[1] You are set apart,[2] and that's final. We do not deserve it, but there is nothing we can do about it but accept it. Mankind and the enemy can try to make us think we are less than what we are. They may say what they will, but they still cannot and never will change what was spoken about us already. The enemy wants to break our hearts every day emotionally and physically in any way he can. So! Let us rise to the occasion and tell him our heart is not his and never will be! We are taken. Along with mankind and the enemy, no job, no organization, not even a friend, dictates your value, your abilities, and skills, or determines if you are "enough."

Regarding your skills, they do not dictate your value or if you are enough either. The only thing that will ever dictate the value of your being is...He was pierced just for you. Your skills are a gift from your Father to you. We can all work at our skills, but we did not create and give them to ourselves. They are not a result of something we did. He only gives good gifts,[3] which means your gift is good. So do not compare your gift to a gift He gave to another, because yours is special too. Because He gave the gift, do not worry about how people respond to your gift. Remember, your value does not change. The world's way is to validate people (or your gift) through recognition, money, status, fame, etc. None of these will ever increase or decrease your value. The enemy will always try to convince you otherwise; that you need these things to validate you.

Regarding opportunities others seem to have, if He has a plan for you, a plan for good, a future and a hope,[4] then do not think you are missing out. Since He made the door, He knows how to open the door for you. Father can do the impossible[5] and make ways where there aren't any, even with the greatest odds against you. It doesn't matter what you look like, what skills you may or may not have, or if you know the right people. If He says so, then it is so. It's as simple as that.

Friend, you were fearfully and wonderfully made,[6] and your identity is in Him. Do not think about what everyone else thinks of you, gets to do, or is accomplishing. Think about what He thinks of you, what He is allowing you to do and, because of this, look at what all you are accomplishing.

With that, you and I have places to be, things to change, and things to conquer.[7] We do not have time to worry about how valuable someone thinks we are, or what they are doing or get to do. We have to let go of this comparison. We have to let go, so *we* can go![8]

--Me

P.S. The King created your whole being and put His signature by it.

90

CHAPTER 21

Sustainment

Mark 4:37 (CSB) A great windstorm arose, and the waves were breaking over the boat, so that the boat was already being swamped.

Acts 27:20 Since neither sun nor stars appeared for many days, and no small storm was assailing *us*, from then on all hope of our being saved was gradually abandoned.

Jeremiah 1:4-5 (CSB) The word of the Lord came to me: I chose you before I formed you in the womb; I set you apart before you were born. I appointed you a prophet to the nations.

Isaiah 43:2 "When you pass through the waters, I will be with you; and through the rivers, they will not overflow you. When you walk through the fire, you will not be scorched, nor will the flame burn you.

Romans 15:4 For whatever was written in earlier times was written for our instruction, so that through perseverance and the encouragement of the Scriptures we might have hope.

Sustainment

Hi Friend,

I was listening to a song, and I could barely get through it because I had this overwhelming desire to encourage you right away. We never thought we would go through any of the things we have gone through or are currently experiencing. I am sure you, along with me, had no idea life would be so hard and sometimes so incredibly cruel. It feels as if it is never-ending. Some days we have just enough to push through with the hope it will not be too much longer for better to come. But then, there are other days where hope is nearly gone and all we can do is cry. We cry because we have pushed, believed, worked hard, had faith, prayed, tried to do everything we are supposed to, yet here we are, and nothing has changed.

My encouragement is not that it will be over tomorrow, but rather that I am in the boat with you, swamped by the same waves,[1] battered[2] by the same storms. I am thankful to share my boat with you. Perhaps we share the same boat (journey), because of what our futures hold, and we need to know who is sailing with us now.

I know it feels as if we are just drifting at sea and cannot see the shore. There must be something going on, because the waves never take us out, they just hit, sting, push, and nearly drown us. Even when the rogue wave sneaks in to destroy us, it never accomplishes its goal, because somehow here we stand.

I just have to think, if He really is the one who determines if we are born into this world, then this means we are here on purpose, and if we are here on purpose, then this is why the waves haven't taken us.

Jesus, here we stand with our feelings of despair, frustration, and tears. The waves hurt and take our breath away sometimes, but You never let them carry us away. Thank You for being the Something going on, for being in the boat too,[3] and allowing us to still stand.

--Me

P.S. Perhaps we should get the nets ready.[4]

CHAPTER 22

Thank You Friend

Philippians 1:3-5 I thank my God in all my remembrance of you, always offering prayer with joy in my every prayer for you all, in view of your participation in the gospel from the first day until now.

John 14:26 But the Helper, the Holy Spirit, whom the Father will send in My name, He will teach you all things, and bring to your remembrance all that I said to you.

Philippians 2:4 do not *merely* look out for your own personal interests, but also for the interests of others.

Galatians 6:2 Bear one another's burdens, and thereby fulfill the law of Christ.

Proverbs 27:9 (CSB) Oil and incense bring joy to the heart, and the sweetness of a friend is better than self-counsel.

Thank You Friend

Hi Friend,

I wanted to tell you words that could show you how thankful I am for you. So, on the way home tonight I ask the Holy Spirit what to say.

When I think of a daughter of God, I think of you. You are so gentle, thoughtful, and genuinely care about others. You actually have a "care team" posture you live out and show all the time.

When I first moved here (I will never forget), you offered to come pick me up for a Bible study, but it was so out of the way for you to do this. I did not understand why you would do this. Then you always hugged me. You also tell all your friends you love them. You showed me a whole new world about loving friends. You still do all of this and, in fact, every word of truth, encouragement, and every way you show empathy is just another hug to me.

For whatever reason Father has intertwined us in this time to help each other, even when we have no clue this is what He is doing. It is weird how He has us helping each other at the same time with both of us going through all of this. It is said that iron sharpens iron.[1]

I am thankful for your life and, the breath He gave you.[2] Thank you for your first hug and all the ones to come. I look forward to the day where we see each other There, and just smile back at each other because we know we made it through.

--Me

P.S. May we look for each other when we get There, so once again we can break bread together and share. Until then, onward we shall!

CHAPTER 23

Kicking Down the Wall for You

1 Chronicles 16:10-11 Glory in His holy name; let the heart of those who seek the LORD be glad. Seek the LORD and His strength; seek His face continually.

Philippians 3:13 Brethren, I do not regard myself as having laid hold of *it* yet; but one thing *I do:* forgetting what *lies* behind and reaching forward to what *lies* ahead,

Joshua 1:9 Have I not commanded you? Be strong and courageous! Do not tremble or be dismayed, for the LORD your God is with you wherever you go."

2 Kings 6:16-17 So he answered, "Do not fear, for those who are with us are more than those who are with them." Then Elisha prayed and said, "O LORD, I pray, open his eyes that he may see." And the LORD opened the servant's eyes and he saw; and behold, the mountain was full of horses and chariots of fire all around Elisha.

2 Chronicles 20:17 You *need* not fight in this *battle;* station yourselves, stand and see the salvation of the LORD on your behalf, O Judah and Jerusalem.' Do not fear or be dismayed; tomorrow go out to face them, for the LORD is with you."

Kicking Down the Wall for You

Hi Friend,

This might be a little strange, but you have been on my heart a lot lately. I keep praying for you for whatever is going on. For some reason, I hurt for you.

I am not sure what this is all about or what is going on, and I do not need to know. I just want to tell you I am here, ready to take the front line, and have my bow arched for you. Whatever the enemy is telling you, tell him what he has coming for him. I feel as if I am supposed to tell you that you are enough, Jesus loves you,[1] and seek Him.

Do not believe lies that you have messed up too much, that you never do anything right, or you will never be what you are supposed to be. We all have done things that are stupid, embarrassing, those "what were we thinking" things, and have not made the best decisions. Unfortunately, this is part of this life, and I hate it. The only thing we can do with these things is let it hurt us or let it help others. Do not look back, and do not let your feelings use the past to determine the present. Our past does not define us. Those seasons do not tell our whole ashes[2] to beautiful stories. The enemy wants us to focus on the land behind so we can't focus on the journey ahead. However, we have a lot of work left to do, so don't let the enemy distract and discourage you, because you are an especially important piece to the puzzle.

The enemy also wants us to think we are all alone, alone in the dark, at a dead-end road. Except he deceives,[3] and all we have to do is kick over the fake wall he places in front of us, so we can see the truth, and see there are others on our path, too. Rest knowing everyone has your back, the ones who love you that you can see, and all the ones you cannot. Know it is okay to fall back a few rows in the battle, and even sit behind a rock, because those who are with us are more than with them.[4] We fight with you; you do not fight alone. I am kicking down the wall for you.

--Me

P.S. The enemy cannot have your fear because Your God has your faith.

CHAPTER 24

Always Enough

Proverbs 14:1 The wise woman builds her house, but the foolish tears it down with her own hands.

Proverbs 31:10-12 An excellent wife, who can find? For her worth is far above jewels. The heart of her husband trusts in her, and he will have no lack of gain. She does him good and not evil all the days of her life.

1 Samuel 16:7 But the LORD said to Samuel, "Do not look at his appearance or at the height of his stature, because I have rejected him; for God *sees* not as man sees, for man looks at the outward appearance, but the LORD looks at the heart."

1 Peter 3:3-4 Your adornment must not be *merely* external--braiding the hair, and wearing gold jewelry, or putting on dresses; but *let it be* the hidden person of the heart, with the imperishable quality of a gentle and quiet spirit, which is precious in the sight of God.

2 Corinthians 2:15 For we are a fragrance of Christ to God among those who are being saved and among those who are perishing;

Always Enough

Hi Friend,

Why is it we struggle so much with feeling good enough or beautiful enough? I know that what we both have been through does not help; but even before those fires, we struggled. I know we are not alone in the struggle and most women struggle with us. A lot of our friends struggle with this in different ways too, and even our guy friends struggle with being enough. For us girls, I think a lot of times these feelings stem from what we see in the mirror. We have this innate desire to be a beauty for an Adam.

But you are more than a beauty for your Adam. You are a suitable helper[1] and help more than with your body. You help in the way you care for, encourage, and point him to the One; the way you help take care of the home and family you built together; the way you hold him when his heart is down, make him laugh, and give him the ability to smile that smile when only you are around.

Beauty is more than what we can see, and anyone seeking Jesus knows it is the heart that is beautiful. This is why kindness, humility, and compassion, will always be more attractive no matter what body it comes through.

I don't think there is anything wrong with wanting to be and feel beautiful, and I know for myself how much I desire this too; but this is not what determines if you are good enough. It isn't even about if you are *sometimes* enough; rather, you are *always* enough.

Why? Because you are His.[2] You were enough when He gave you His breath and brought you forth to life.[3] You were enough when He came and searched just for you,[4] and you were enough when He took His last breath[5] thinking of you. He chose you out of the world to be His.[6] You are always enough because He demonstrated so, and says so, and this is beautiful. You are beautiful too. When He looked at all creation that He made and saw it was very good indeed,[7] He saw you. He sees your internal adornment of your heart, which is precious in His sight.[8] And because He gave and saved, you are a beautiful fragrance of Jesus[9] forever and always.

--Me

P.S. You are a crown.[10]

CHAPTER 25

Out of the Valley

Psalm 115:1 Not to us, O LORD, not to us, but to Your name give glory because of Your lovingkindness, because of Your truth.

Psalm 116:3-5 The cords of death encompassed me and the terrors of Sheol came upon me; I found distress and sorrow. Then I called upon the name of the LORD: "O LORD, I beseech You, save my life!" Gracious is the LORD, and righteous; Yes, our God is compassionate.

Romans 8:28 And we know that God causes all things to work together for good to those who love God, to those who are called according to *His* purpose.

Psalm 30:2 O LORD my God, I cried to You for help, and You healed me.

John 8:58 Jesus said to them, "Truly, truly, I say to you, before Abraham was born, I am."

Out of the Valley

Friends,

Hi. I decided to send a letter to all of you because I want to thank you for something and give Jesus glory for something. Also, a text would have been way too long, so a letter it was.

There is a certain day coming up and, although it may seem like an ordinary day, to me it marks the day my life was changed forever. I want to thank all of you, for all of the support, kind words, prayers, and the time you gave me in the last two years. It certainly was horrific and the level above pain, but He used you all to help me, and I am so appreciative! Thank you, to all of you from my whole heart.

My story has been rough, but maybe it will not always be. Maybe my story is Job's story, where the second part of my life will be better than the first.[1] Or maybe my story is Joseph's story, where I started out in the pit but end up in places and spaces only my Father can orchestrate.[2] Or perhaps I have my own story--who knows? What I do know is that in the last two years, even though it started out as death and ashes, it has slowly evolved to the groundbreaking open and a stem appearing.

My Father has shown so much of His grace, love, and compassion towards me in this time, and He has done some incredible things both big and small—too many to list here. I know you already know of and have witnessed some of these things He has done. He has done things for me which cannot be explained and made seemingly impossible ways happen, and has even put me in places and spaces only He can. Every area of my life seems to be better and moving forward. It is as if He worked all things out for my good[3] because I love Him. I think my ashes are getting ready to take shape into beauty[4] as my stem that has appeared, has been growing, and is getting ready to bloom. I know it sounds silly, but it is true.

How is this possible? Through all the nights screaming out and weeping in pain, how can it turn out to be like this? Could it be, He is truly real? He is near to the brokenhearted,[5] He is Healer,[6] Comforter,[7] Teacher,[8] Forgiver,[9] Provider,[10] Restorer,[11] Peace[12]… He said it Himself: "I Am".[13] He has to be, there is no other way to explain it.

109

Revelation 5:13 "I heard every creature in heaven, on earth, under the earth, on the sea, and everything in them say, Blessing and honor and glory and power be to the one seated on the throne, and to the Lamb, forever and ever!"

Thank You Jesus, for everything You brought me through. Yours is[14] because You are forever.

--Me

P.S. I wonder what kind of flower will bloom from my stem.

CHAPTER 26

Diamonds

James 1:19-20 *This* you know, my beloved brethren. But everyone must be quick to hear, slow to speak *and* slow to anger; for the anger of man does not achieve the righteousness of God.

John 8:12 Then Jesus again spoke to them, saying, "I am the Light of the world; he who follows Me will not walk in the darkness, but will have the Light of life."

Romans 12:1-2 Therefore I urge you, brethren, by the mercies of God, to present your bodies a living and holy sacrifice, acceptable to God, *which is* your spiritual service of worship. And do not be conformed to this world, but be transformed by the renewing of your mind, so that you may prove what the will of God is, that which is good and acceptable and perfect.

Hebrews 13:9 Do not be carried away by varied and strange teachings; for it is good for the heart to be strengthened by grace, not by foods, through which those who were so occupied were not benefited.

Philippians 2:14-16 (CSB) Do everything without grumbling and arguing, so that you may be blameless and pure, children of God who are faultless in a crooked and perverted generation, among whom you shine like stars in the world, by holding firm to the word of life. Then I can boast in the day of Christ that I didn't run or labor for nothing.

Diamonds

Part 1

Hi Friends,

The world seems to be falling apart today, where we are seeing brother against brother and sister against sister. It is a really soul-wrenching scene, and the world desperately needs to see there is Light.[1] Today is the day the Lord has made though,[2] and it is a good time to be bold, speaking with the truth in love,[3] with the renewing of our minds.[4] Where being bold with the renewing of our mind right now is not looked at favorably and will cause us to be under immense pressure. We have to step back out of the world, setting our minds on things above,[5] and step out of our own pain, and try to see what He sees and do what He says. We have to take hold of the words He says; do not be conformed to this world.[6] If we look around and see how the world is responding right now, and we do not follow the crowds, then we automatically are under immense pressure for Jesus. It is okay though because we have the same Spirit in us, a Spirit not of fear but of power, love and of sound judgement.[7] We can't look like the crowd, because how else will they see. So, let us not join in what the world is doing, let us not be led astray,[8] so we can know what His good and perfect will[9] is for each and every day.

The fight is not against flesh,[10] it is against the enemy, and it always has been. If we recognize this and show love to all,[11] guilty or not, in action and truth,[12] then we will be the diamonds set apart that people in the chaotic patterns of this world can see shine and can look to for truth. We cannot just speak things and not speak Him. Let us remind each other what His Word says, because all of His words are profitable for teaching, rebuking, correcting, and training us in righteousness.[13] Let us also encourage one another like Paul and the author of Hebrews says, as the day draws near.[14] Today is the day the Lord has made,[15] and it is a good time to be bold, speaking with the truth in love,[16] speaking *Him*, the only thing that will change anything. The only thing that can break the patterns. Let us be His weapons for righteousness,[17] soldiers for Jesus Christ.[18] Let us shine.

--Me

P.S. May we turn our eyes upon Jesus.[19]

1 Timothy 2:1-6 First of all, then, I urge that entreaties *and* prayers, petitions *and* thanksgivings, be made on behalf of all men, for kings and all who are in authority, so that we may lead a tranquil and quiet life in all godliness and dignity. This is good and acceptable in the sight of God our Savior, who desires all men to be saved and to come to the knowledge of the truth. For there is one God, *and* one mediator also between God and men, *the* man Christ Jesus, who gave Himself as a ransom for all, the testimony *given* at the proper time.

Titus 3:1-2 Remind them to be subject to rulers, to authorities, to be obedient, to be ready for every good deed, to malign no one, to be peaceable, gentle, showing every consideration for all men.

Romans 12:9-10 *Let* love *be* without hypocrisy. Abhor what is evil; cling to what is good. *Be* devoted to one another in brotherly love; give preference to one another in honor;

Psalm 143:10 Teach me to do Your will, for You are my God; let Your good Spirit lead me on level ground.

2 Chronicles 30:8 (CSB) Don't become obstinate now like your ancestors did. Give your allegiance to the LORD, and come to his sanctuary that he has consecrated forever. Serve the LORD your God so that he may turn his burning anger away from you,

Diamonds

Part 2

Father, Jesus, Holy Spirit,

Thank You.

Father, I pray for a movement against all evil. I pray for a movement towards You, towards true Love.[1] You tell us to pray for our enemies,[2] for all in authority,[3] and for each other.[4]

Father, Your Word says Your Spirit made us and You gave us Your breath.[5] Please help us see no one person's breath is more valuable than the other, because it is all the same breath–Yours. I pray for our enemies. That their needs could be met, and for them to know You are real. I pray for their salvation if they have not already accepted You. I pray they will seek You with everything they are. Please help us know how to do good to our enemies[6] and not be glad when something bad happens to them,[7] as You tell us to do. Please help us to not seek out vengeance, because You say it belongs to You.[8]

I pray for all those You put in authority at every level, political, military, and law enforcement. I pray their needs could be met, for them to know You are real, for their salvation if they have not already accepted You. I pray they will seek after Your heart, so their hearts can know how to make decisions for our hearts. That they will have the courage to still do the task You put in front of them. For wisdom and guidance, for protection, for honor for all threats averted and lives saved that will never be talked about or shared. I pray we all would try to take the lead honoring one another[9] like You say, even showing it to them.

Father, I pray for Your people, we who know Your voice,[10] that our needs could be met, and that we seek You with everything we are. Please guide us and help us point others only to You and nothing else. Please remind us a harsh word stirs up wrath, but a gentle word turns away anger.[11] Please help us understand how to do whatever we can on our part to keep the peace,[12] and please help us let righteousness lead and not our flesh and pain. Please help us see that if we pledge our allegiance to You, then we cannot dishonor in one space to try to gain honor in another. Please help us all read Your words, and understand Your definition of things, so we know what to do. Please help us conquer evil with good,[13] as we hang on to the hope of Your coming day.[14]

Father, Jesus, Holy Spirit, I love You and I honor You.

--Me

P.S. Help us look full into Your wonderful face.[15]

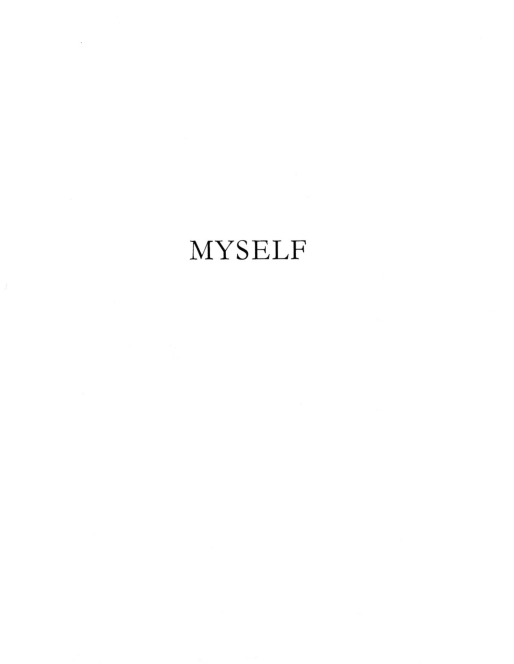

MYSELF

CHAPTER 27

He is Good

Psalm 34:19 Many are the afflictions of the righteous, but the LORD delivers him out of them all.

Psalm 18:19 (HCSB) He brought me out to a spacious place; He rescued me because He delighted in me.

Psalm 4:3 But know that the LORD has set apart the godly man for Himself; the LORD hears when I call to Him.

Psalm 73:23 Nevertheless I am continually with You; You have taken hold of my right hand.

Psalm 136:1 Give thanks to the LORD, for He is good, for His lovingkindness is everlasting.

He is Good

Self,

I know sometimes in the tough moments when it looks as if He is not there, when the storms come and rip up the trees and throw debris (life) all around. When everything looks like chaos, and when the water rises and there is just enough room to breathe, you start to wonder and question things. But do you ever sit back and wonder, how every time when the storm comes and it looks grave, you always step out and walk away?

Maybe when you start to question and negativity comes about, you can throw it overboard to lighten the load, and remember all the times you have walked away because of His grace, protection, and love for you. How he took your hand and showed you out of the pit[1]; how He always makes a way in the waters[2]; how your foot has not slipped.[3] Those are just the things you know He did and does for you. I bet there are many more you will never know about; many arrows you will never see.

Do you remember the other day when you realized He really did bring you to a spacious place, a safe spacious place[4] to wait out the season of in-between? How He has helped you, sustained you, stood in the fire with you, even though He didn't have to?

Even before He did all of this, may I remind you, He took a moment of His time to create you. He took His breath and breathed it inside of you.[5] He chose you out of the world[6] and set you apart for Himself.[7] He saved you by taking His last breath for you.[8] He loved the world,[9] stopped the world as it was known, and gave His Only so all who would believe could live for eternity.[10] He stopped the world just for you.

Don't you see He has always been holding on to you, protecting you, caring for you, loving you? After all, He included you and wrote all your days in His book.[11] He is good and good to you.

--Me

P.S. Do you ever wonder if sometimes those little neat things that happen in your life, if He orchestrates them just to see you smile?

CHAPTER 28

Keep Going

Psalm 38:17 For I am ready to fall, and my sorrow is continually before me.

Psalm 88:9 My eye has wasted away because of affliction; I have called upon You every day, O LORD; I have spread out my hands to You.

Job 6:11 (CSB) What strength do I have, that I should continue to hope? What is my future, that I should be patient?

1 Kings 19:7 (HCSB) Then the angel of the LORD returned for a second time and touched him. He said, "Get up and eat, or the journey will be too much for you."

Psalm 27:13-14 *I would have despaired* unless I had believed that I would see the goodness of the LORD in the land of the living. Wait for the LORD; be strong and let your heart take courage; yes, wait for the LORD.

Keep Going

Self,

I know you are struggling with the question: what is the point? What is the point to keep going with life? You feel like you are living some weird *Groundhog Day* movie, where day in and day out nothing changes. It's the same scene over and over. You wake up, feel the pain, go to bed. The same day, the same pain, the song that never ends.[1]

I know you are wondering why He still isn't allowing you to go home and be with Him. If He didn't take you then, He isn't going to take you now. For Him to allow you to go through all you did, and after you begged Him to take you…and then for Him to take you now? No. He didn't take You out of the bad just to leave you in the woods. I know it hurts. I know you want it to stop. I know you have been seeking Him and telling Him how you feel. I know sometimes the hope is gone. I know you always hear that He has a plan for you, that a breakthrough is right around the corner, and if you still have breath then He isn't done with you. After hearing this for so long, you wonder sometimes if you are just lying to yourself, if those things are true for you.

Well, if He isn't going to leave you in the woods, and the woods (wilderness) was not the end to the Israelites' story, then this isn't the end of your story either. So how much longer do you have to live in this scene? I do not know. I do know however, these thoughts of giving up, thoughts of defeat, thoughts of "what is the point", are all attacks meant to harm you and to take you out, attacks by the enemy. They are meant to steal, kill and destroy you,[2] to keep you from getting to where you are supposed to be. Don't believe him. Don't let the enemy squeeze the life out of you.

For now, you need to get up and eat, because the journey may be long[3] but will be worth it. The promised land is out ahead.[4] Put on that armor[5] because right now this is war. Put on the words He has spoken and write them on your arms and legs. Write out and hang prayers, truth, and life on the wall. Remember you have the Spirit of power,[6] and command anything not of Jesus to leave from you. Ask Jesus to do a Lazarus[7] and bring life back to the bones of your hope. Keep holding your head up even though the tears fall down. Keep screaming His name out loud, keep reading, keep asking, keep seeking, keep knocking,[8] keep listening, keep believing, keep fighting, and keep breathing. Keep going because what was, was, and now is now. There is no turning back. Listen to your own saying "Steady the ship of your mind, arch the bow of your heart, and take hold of the Hand already taking hold of you".

Your fighting will add up. When the day comes where the next scene is played, there all your efforts to keep fighting will be, and there will be victory. He is undefeated, and as He is, so are you in this world.[9]

Remember others know how you feel and have felt this too. Paul said when they were in Asia that they despaired of life.[10] Also, remember even Jesus said His soul was swallowed up in sorrow, to the point of death.[11] But they did not give up, they kept going.

This isn't the end to your story—it never was. If He is the Creator of your breath, and He has not played the ending credits yet, then how can you? Pick up your arrows and keep going.

--Me

P.S. A few years of the good fight, eternity for the good life. Your momentary afflictions have nothing on what is to come.[12]

CHAPTER 29

Out at Sea

1 Peter 1:13 Therefore, prepare your minds for action, keep sober *in spirit,* fix your hope completely on the grace to be brought to you at the revelation of Jesus Christ.

Psalm 91:11 For He will give His angels charge concerning you, to guard you in all your ways.

Deuteronomy 31:6 Be strong and courageous, do not be afraid or tremble at them, for the LORD your God is the one who goes with you. He will not fail you or forsake you."

Isaiah 40:29 He gives strength to the weary, and to *him who* lacks might He increases power.

2 Kings 2:8 Elijah took his mantle and folded it together and struck the waters, and they were divided here and there, so that the two of them crossed over on dry ground.

Out at Sea

Self,

I see you there floating out at sea, looking for the shore (hope). I know it has been rough, trying to swim towards the shore but not exactly sure where it is. I know you feel like the enemy (sharks) can attack at any moment. Don't forget He has His angels (school of fish) surrounding you and hiding you from the enemy. I know you get stung by people (jellyfish) from time to time, but He always sends help (dolphins) to hold you up when you feel like you can't swim any longer. When fear, worry, anxiety, feelings of defeat and any other lie come swimming your way, just remember He can speak and cause megalodon to rise up and devour those sharks. So don't be afraid. I know the journey of life (waves) can get rough and exhausting and even sometimes scary, because you can't see what is out ahead.

I also know you wish there could be an easier way, and you feel as if you will sink if you don't keep kicking. I know it is a fight to keep swimming.

I just have one question for you though. I am not sure why you are struggling so hard out there in the water, because if you have that same Power within you,[1] and faith even as a mustard seed,[2] can you not just strike the waters[3] too and walk the rest of the way to the shore?

--Me

P.S. I'm just saying...

CHAPTER 30

Loneliness

Psalm 102:4-7 My heart has been smitten like grass and has withered away, indeed, I forget to eat my bread. Because of the loudness of my groaning my bones cling to my flesh. I resemble a pelican of the wilderness; I have become like an owl of the waste places. I lie awake, I have become like a lonely bird on a housetop.

Psalm 25:16-18 Turn to me and be gracious to me, for I am lonely and afflicted. The troubles of my heart are enlarged; bring me out of my distresses. Look upon my affliction and my trouble, and forgive all my sins.

Psalm 62:5 My soul, wait in silence for God only, for my hope is from Him.

Revelation 3:20 Behold, I stand at the door and knock; if anyone hears My voice and opens the door, I will come in to him and will dine with him, and he with Me.

Psalm 34:18 The LORD is near to the brokenhearted and saves those who are crushed in spirit.

Loneliness

Self,

I hope you are doing well, but I know you are not. Some days are better than others, and some days like today are just plain excruciating. Father has brought you out of some devastating fires and the smoke has settled, but I know it is lonely here. I know you are trying to trust this time has to be. You wonder why you are so lonely and sad, and wonder if these feelings mean you do not have faith. But faith isn't the absence of feelings. Wouldn't it make more sense that faith is looking to Him in the midst of the feelings? In the midst of the hurt, uncertainty, and loneliness where the tears never end, you still look at Him, and talk to Him, knowing if there is any hope, it comes from Him?

I know this season of your life does not feel like a time of peace and quiet, a retreat away from the noise, but instead a relentless, never-ending, solitary, silent place--a place, where day in and day out it is just you, the silence, and the stares off into space. A place where your eyes open in the morning and you realize nothing has changed. A place where there is no one to say good morning to, see their smile, and encourage for the day. No one to text just "because," or tell about something exciting that happened, or vent to when something did not go as planned. No one to make dinner plans with, cook with, or break bread with. No one to share movie night or watch a favorite show with. No joke to tell or laugh to laugh. No one to pray over, kiss good-night, and rest with. No one to run errands with, take a trip with, or hold hands with. No birthday parties or holiday gatherings. No decorating the tree or baking holiday cookies. No one to hold or to hold you in the tears, pain, or when sick. No one to support in the battle or to celebrate the victories. No one to help make hard decisions or help fix things around the house. Simply no one to do life with.

I know you wonder all the time when or if this will ever go away, and your heart hurts for those who truly understand. I would say to you, and to all of those who do understand, that all you can do is continue. Continue to wake up and say good morning to Him, see His smile for you and let Him encourage you. Continue to talk to Him just "because," or tell Him about the exciting or painful events that come about. Continue to ask Him what is for dinner

133

and break bread with Him. Invite Him to watch the movie or show. Tell Him jokes and listen to His. Continue to kiss Him good-night as you pray and He prays over you, as you rest in Him. Talk to Him in the grocery stores and let Him hold your hand. Celebrate His birthday and let Him celebrate yours. Decorate His tree while He shows you how to bake the best cookies. Let Him hold you through the tears and heal you from the pain and sickness. Continue to remember He is with you in the battle and He celebrates your victories. Ask Him His opinion with the hard decisions and let Him show you how to fix the things around the house. Simply continue to do life with Him.

--Me

P.S. Keep trusting this season has to be, and You are not alone because He is with you.[1] If the eyes of Your Lord are everywhere,[2] don't you think He sees you too? So, continue on because you do not know what He has in store for you.

CHAPTER 31

The Woods

Psalm 55:6-7 I said, "Oh, that I had wings like a dove! I would fly away and be at rest. "Behold, I would wander far away, I would lodge in the wilderness. Selah.

Exodus 13:21-22 The LORD was going before them in a pillar of cloud by day to lead them on the way, and in a pillar of fire by night to give them light, that they might travel by day and by night. He did not take away the pillar of cloud by day, nor the pillar of fire by night, from before the people.

Exodus 16:4 Then the LORD said to Moses, "Behold, I will rain bread from heaven for you; and the people shall go out and gather a day's portion every day, that I may test them, whether or not they will walk in My instruction.

Job 33:14 (CSB) For God speaks time and again, but a person may not notice it.

Numbers 20:8 "Take the rod; and you and your brother Aaron assemble the congregation and speak to the rock before their eyes, that it may yield its water. You shall thus bring forth water for them out of the rock and let the congregation and their beasts drink."

The Woods

Self,

(Sigh) It is storming again… I guess I will sit here at the base of this tree, with my knees to my chest and head on my knees. It seems as if it storms all the time out here, and I have been out here for a while. I thought this was the "in-between" but now I am not so sure. It seems as if I have traveled millions of miles, but maybe not; it all seems like a blur. If only David *and* I had wings like a bird, except I would not stay in the wilderness, but far I would flee.[1] Maybe I'd find my way out of here, fly above the trees, find rest, find some milk and honey.[2] I don't know.

How come I can't find my way out of here? Am I even going the right way? What if I have just been going in circles? Am I making this take longer than it was supposed to by years instead of days? How do I **get out of here**!? I know these are the same thoughts as yesterday, but lately it just seems like nothing will ever change. I don't know.

(Sitting at the base of the tree, making up a song while playing with a stick) Be though as it may, the storm clouds will eventually go away… won't they? Then what? Because here I will still be wandering around the woods… perhaps the way out is just beyond this tree?… I feel so alone, with just my thoughts, my tears, and my uncertainty. Although there is this one weird Cloud[3] which seems to never go away. And what is this stuff that keeps falling on the ground every day?[4] I don't know.

I keep asking, as I walk through these woods, for Him to show me He is near[5] in a way I can see, because I *want to see Him move*--desperately. Yesterday when I asked, I didn't see anything except a momma deer and her baby come run up beside me. Sometimes I wonder if His ear is even attentive to His little sheep.[6] If He *is* listening to me, why doesn't He say anything? All I can hear is water falling from these rocks.[7] I just wish He would speak. I don't know.

You know, sometimes it feels like someone is holding my hand,[8] like an invisible friend who is leading me[9]…that sounds pretty crazy…I don't know. There are also those moments when I feel as if something is following close behind me. I guess I don't mind because it feels like something good, something like mercy.[10] It is weird at night too, how I always stay warm, like a fire[11] is going, even when it storms. I don't know how I always fall asleep out here, all alone in the dark, I guess I feel covered,[12] and feel encamped[13] with safety[14] and peace[15] guarding my heart? Perhaps it could be worse out here in the woods. There could be snakes or giants chasing after me. Now if I could just figure out how come in the mornings there always seems to be feathers on me[16]... I don't know.

I don't know what to do anymore. I think I am just going to get up and follow this Cloud and see where it leads.

--Me

P.S. Is it weird that the Cloud is stopping at the sea?[17]

CHAPTER 32

Game Over

Ephesians 6:14-15 Stand firm therefore, HAVING GIRDED YOUR LOINS WITH TRUTH, and HAVING PUT ON THE BREASTPLATE OF RIGHTEOUSNESS, and having shod YOUR FEET WITH THE PREPARATION OF THE GOSPEL OF PEACE;

Psalm 144:1 Blessed be the LORD, my rock, who trains my hands for war, *and* my fingers for battle;

Revelation 20:10 And the devil who deceived them was thrown into the lake of fire and brimstone, where the beast and the false prophet are also; and they will be tormented day and night forever and ever.

1 John 5:3-5 For this is the love of God, that we keep His commandments; and His commandments are not burdensome. For whatever is born of God overcomes the world; and this is the victory that has overcome the world-- our faith. Who is the one who overcomes the world, but he who believes that Jesus is the Son of God?

Matthew 16:18 (KJV) "And I say also unto thee, that thou art Peter, and upon this rock I will build my church; and the gates of hell shall not prevail against it."

Game Over

Self,

One, two, you better buckle those shoes. Three, four, this is war. Five, six, don't believe his tricks.

Seven, eight…You already know his fate. Nine, ten, Jesus told you, you would win!

--Me

P.S Eleven, twelve, the gates of Hell will not prevail![1]

CHAPTER 33

Future Life

1 John 1:5 This is the message we have heard from Him and announce to you, that God is Light, and in Him there is no darkness at all.

Colossians 2:6-7 Therefore as you have received Christ Jesus the Lord, *so* walk in Him, having been firmly rooted *and now* being built up in Him and established in your faith, just as you were instructed, *and* overflowing with gratitude.

Psalm 31:19 How great is Your goodness, which You have stored up for those who fear You, which You have wrought for those who take refuge in You, before the sons of men!

John 10:10 The thief comes only to steal and kill and destroy; I came that they may have life, and have *it* abundantly.

James 5:11 We count those blessed who endured. You have heard of the endurance of Job and have seen the outcome of the Lord's dealings, that the Lord is full of compassion and *is* merciful.

Future Life

Self,

Behold, a flower. A flower just for you. I know you are hurting now, but I want you to know soon there will be flowers all around. I know it has been a long time coming to see the blooms. What started out seeming like death was just a seed needing to be bandaged, nurtured, and to rest. Seeking more of the Water[1] and Light,[2] the seed gained strength and realized to finally be strong and to grow only in Him,[3] the Resurrection and the Life,[4] the Truth.[5] The barrier was broken through where all started to see you, the same *you* which had always been but awakened and strengthened. The storms came while you were growing and healing, but you were firmly rooted in Him.[6] Now watch because the bloom is opening, and once again you will see all His never-ending goodness and faithfulness,[7] His grace.[8] All the glory to Him.[9]

Thank you for every time you keep going and pushing through even when you just don't want to. I pray the voyage of tears ends here, so that soon you can clearly see all there is to see. I cannot wait for you to see what your future will be. Behold, a flower just for you, from Him who gives abundantly.[10]

--Me

P.S. I have heard of Job's endurance and his outcome. The Lord is very compassionate and merciful.[11]

OTHERS

CHAPTER 34

What Jesus Says

Psalm 145:9 (CSB) The Lord is good to everyone; his compassion rests on all he has made.

Psalm 104:21 The young lions roar after their prey and seek their food from God.

Genesis 9:9-10 "Now behold, I Myself do establish My covenant with you, and with your descendants after you; and with every living creature that is with you, the birds, the cattle, and every beast of the earth with you; of all that comes out of the ark, even every beast of the earth.

Psalm 50:10-12 "For every beast of the forest is Mine, the cattle on a thousand hills. "I know every bird of the mountains, and everything that moves in the field is Mine. "If I were hungry I would not tell you, for the world is Mine, and all it contains.

Proverbs 12:10 (HCSB) A righteous man cares about his animal's health, but even the merciful acts of the wicked are cruel.

What Jesus Says

Animals,

I have been in awe of you ever since I can remember. I have always been trying to talk to, touch, catch, and help you. When I was younger, I would even have dreams about you. One in particular was about you, eagle. I can remember I was talking with you and asked you if you knew Jesus. It is weird how you animals have always been on my mind, even as a kid in my dreams. I can remember the first one of you birdies I rescued as an "experienced" five-year-old. You and your mate were sitting in the road. At the time, I was not sure what was wrong but I knew you couldn't fly. So, I went and picked you up. Then I got in *big* trouble because I touched you and was told to let you go. Little did anyone know, that *would not* be the last time I would do this.

I feel for you all in ways I do not with anything else. I can feel the most excitement or the most pain coming from my most inner being. I will never understand why there is such a fight to show you all compassion and love. His compassion rests on all He has made,[1] and the earth is full of His love.[2]

There are over 1500 mentions, including over 120 species of you,[3] written in the Word, even with parts of the very first chapter dedicated to you, speaking of your creation. And, it also says that after your Creator created you, He saw that it was good.[4]

He sees you birdies and says that not one of you is forgotten in His sight.[5] He causes the grass to grow for you livestock,[6] and waters to flow for all of you wild beast.[7] He provides for you, even when you roar[8] and cry out to Him,[9] and in the sea you wait for Him to provide at the right time and are satisfied with good things.[10] He satisfies the desire of every living thing.[11]

He preserves you along with man[12] and even saved you from being completely wiped away by the flood.[13] He tells us several times that He made a covenant with you, and the rainbow in the clouds is for you, too.[14]

He has made it clear to us that you are His: each and every one of you in the forests, on the hills, in the mountains, and in the fields.[15] I wonder if we would take better care of you if we believed and remembered this. He cares how we treat you, and says the righteous cares about his animals health.[16] He

151

tells us to know the condition of our flocks and to pay attention to our herds.[17] That if our brother's donkey or ox has fallen on the road, we must help get you up.[18] Or if we see you lying helpless under your load, and you belong to someone who hates us, we must not refrain from helping you.[19] He told Moses when an ox, sheep, or goat is born, it must stay with its mother for seven days.[20] He told Jonah He cared for the people and animals in Nineveh.[21] He also tells us, after six days of work, we need to let you rest.[22]

Many times, we humans are talked about as His sheep,[23] flock and lambs.[24] Not only are we referred to as you, but He also gives us examples of you to learn from and has used you to help us. Examples such as how you ants work hard, yet we are lazy,[25] and you birds know how to migrate, yet we do not know His requirements.[26] He gave you the donkey a voice to speak to Balaam,[27] used you big fish for Jonah,[28] and you ravens to feed Elijah.[29]

I know there were a lot of sacrifices of you in the Old Testament, but it wasn't that you were just disposable or insignificant, because in order for something to be a sacrifice, then something of value has to be given. You were not sacrificed with no care for your life. When the son of Shelomith got into a fight with the Israelite man, your Creator told Moses that if one of you was killed, restitution had to be given for your life,[30] because you are valuable.

Your Creator even describes Himself like you, sometimes with wings,[31] like an eagle,[32] as the Lamb,[33] or a Dove.[34] He says you will honor Him,[35] and Job told us humans to ask you who has done all this, and you will tell us Who.[36]

Not only are you talked about in this life and in this world, but you were revealed with the Heavenly army when Elisha's servants' eyes were opened, and he saw all the horses and chariots of fire.[37] Also, Isaiah talks about how you all will be together and will rest with each other[38] in a coming time.

It is written that every creature will praise Him.[39] We all, creation and those of us who have the Spirit, eagerly wait for Him to come again.[40]

I don't know, maybe it is just me, but it seems like He kind of likes you. After all, the Lion of Judah[41] will be returning on a white horse[42] with an army behind Him--all on white horses, too.[43]

--Kristen

P.S. And Heaven and nature sing.[44]

CHAPTER 35

My Baby

Psalm 104:24 (CSB) How countless are your works, LORD! In wisdom you have made them all; the earth is full of your creatures.

Ecclesiastes 3:19 For the fate of the sons of men and the fate of beasts is the same. As one dies so dies the other; indeed, they all have the same breath and there is no advantage for man over beast, for all is vanity.

James 1:17 Every good thing given and every perfect gift is from above, coming down from the Father of lights, with whom there is no variation or shifting shadow.

Psalm 66:19-20 But certainly God has heard; He has given heed to the voice of my prayer. Blessed be God, who has not turned away my prayer nor His lovingkindness from me.

Revelation 5:13 (CSB) I heard every creature in heaven, on earth, under the earth, on the sea, and everything in them say, Blessing and honor and glory and power be to the one seated on the throne, and to the Lamb, forever and ever!

My Baby

Baby,

You have been gone for four years now, yet my heart still hurts for you and longs to see you soon. I ask Your Creator and my Father all the time, if He could tell you hello for me and I love you. I still have a picture of you and me beside my bed. Even though the people around me did not quite understand how my love for you was and is, as my dog, they accepted it and knew when you left that a part of me left, too.

Sixteen years we breathed the Creator's breath[1] together. I truly believe with all my being you were a gift. That you were picked and set aside, a good gift[2] just for me. Sometimes when I think of you, a tear still may fall. It may fall because I think of the times where lots of tears would fall and you would be right there trying to comfort me. You would keep giving me kisses until I stopped crying or lay next to me as I tried to breathe. Every morning you would come to the kitchen and eat breakfast with me. You would always wait at the top of the stairs for me. When your tummy was upset, you and I always knew, and we would go outside and I would pick the grass for you. We would play hide and seek, chase each other, and just be silly. I remember those special moments like the moments when I would wake up and you would be lying on me. Even when your eyes and ears failed you, you still knew it was me when I would come home, because you could smell me and would come love on me. You were always with me, beside me, in every activity.

After you left, I struggled with thoughts of how I failed you, that I could have taken better care of you. Everyone says nice things, such as you lived as long as you did because of how well I took care of you. But for me, I will always feel like I could have done better for you. I also struggled with your Creator because He took you from me, but I realized He actually answered a prayer I always prayed for you. The prayer that you would not die alone when the time came, and I could be holding you. So, when I think back on that moment, when I felt and heard your last breath, He answered my prayer. How can I be upset with Him?

I hope now you are having the time of your life because you can see, hear, walk, and run again. I hope you are chasing all the lawn mowers, playing with all your buddies, and happily greeting everyone you see as a friend, as you always did. Even though I hurt here, I know they are blessed to have you there.

Even though I was upset at your Creator for taking you away, I have learned you are His[3] and have always been. How kind He is to have let me share my life with you, and for answering my prayer for when it was time for you to go, I could be holding you. I cannot wait to see and hold you again as we praise Him[4] our Creator and King.

--Me

P.S. I miss you.

CHAPTER 36

Partners Not in Crime

Matthew 13:45-46 "Again, the kingdom of heaven is like a merchant seeking fine pearls, and upon finding one pearl of great value, he went and sold all that he had and bought it.

Revelation 7:9-10 After these things I looked, and behold, a great multitude which no one could count, from every nation and *all* tribes and peoples and tongues, standing before the throne and before the Lamb, clothed in white robes, and palm branches *were* in their hands; and they cry out with a loud voice, saying, "Salvation to our God who sits on the throne, and to the Lamb."

Ephesians 4:15-16 but speaking the truth in love, we are to grow up in all aspects into Him who is the head, *even* Christ, from whom the whole body, being fitted and held together by what every joint supplies, according to the proper working of each individual part, causes the growth of the body for the building up of itself in love.

Psalm 107:14-16 (HCSB) He brought them out of darkness and gloom and broke their chains apart. Let them give thanks to the LORD for His faithful love and His wonderful works for all humanity. For He has broken down the bronze gates and cut through the iron bars.

Hebrews 12:1-2 Therefore, since we have so great a cloud of witnesses surrounding us, let us also lay aside every encumbrance and the sin which so easily entangles us, and let us run with endurance the race that is set before us, fixing our eyes on Jesus, the author and perfecter of faith, who for the joy set before Him endured the cross, despising the shame, and has sat down at the right hand of the throne of God.

Partners Not in Crime

Friend,

I just wanted to remind you: you are not on the mission alone. Sometimes it can feel like a hard, lonely road; but you are not alone. The enemy knows exactly what to say to us and how to make things look like something when they are not. We know he only deceives.[1] There are others of us stationed not far from you, just down this narrow road.

I like to think of us who are on the mission together as a big puzzle--with each of us as a piece of the puzzle. That when we come together, we connect and strengthen one another. I know the puzzle we are in can seem over-whelming, but it is okay because He knows where all the pieces go. We need each other to complete the puzzle, so we will be able to go into all the areas of the world[2] and help each other in every way.[3]

So, know you are not alone, and you are a valuable piece of the puzzle, part of the precious pearl.[4] You are His treasured one.[5] Wherever you are in this world, whatever country, tribe, wherever in all creation, and whatever piece He designed you to be, I just want to thank you. Thank you for doing your piece of the puzzle, for all your examples for us, encouragement for us, prayers for us, support for us, holding firm to the truth for us, and using your gifts and abilities for the Kingdom. Thank you for strengthening us, the puz-zle, which when complete is the picture of Jesus. We are the body.[6] Let us continue to build each other up,[7] pray for each other,[8] and remember we are in this together[9] wherever our station may be. I pray He can help us all breathe the breath of this life, as we run this race that lies before us.[10]

--Kristen

P.S. Oh, and the next time it seems like the enemy has us in chains, let us be sure to check the lock. It could just appear to be locked, but actually be broken[11]--because he only deceives.[12]

CHAPTER 37

Helping Animals

1 Peter 4:10 As each one has received a *special* gift, employ it in serving one another as good stewards of the manifold grace of God.

Hebrews 4:13 (HCSB) No creature is hidden from Him, but all things are naked and exposed to the eyes of Him to whom we must give an account.

John 14:26 But the Helper, the Holy Spirit, whom the Father will send in My name, He will teach you all things, and bring to your remembrance all that I said to you.

Mark 16:15 And He said to them, "Go into all the world and preach the gospel to all creation.

Isaiah 11:6-7 And the wolf will dwell with the lamb, and the leopard will lie down with the young goat, and the calf and the young lion and the fatling together; and a little boy will lead them. Also the cow and the bear will graze, their young will lie down together, and the lion will eat straw like the ox.

Helping Animals

To Those Designed to Help with Animals,

I just want to thank you for what you do for His creation. No matter what area you are in, whether you work with the leaps of the sea, flaps of the air, trots of the field, creeps on the ground, rustles of the forest, or anything in-between, thank you. Not only are we partners *not* in crime for Him with preaching His Word and gathering those to Him, we are also partners designed to help with animals.

Father has given all of us gifts and abilities in different areas,[1] and we are to use them to serve one another.[2] We are the church.[3] There are a lot of needs all over the world and they all look different. Father knows all the needs, even the hidden ones.[4] Perhaps our gifts and abilities look different because all the needs are different.

In the area of animals, the needs and suffering is grave. Our fallen world has been detrimental to animals, and they suffer because of it, and in ways most will never realize or know about. There are things some of us have seen and done for these creatures which are beyond hard. One of my unfortunate but favorite organizations, (unfortunate because I wish they didn't have to exist), is Animal Recovery Mission (ARM).[5] They get involved and help with some of the most horrific situations I have seen. Be prepared to brace yourself for what you'll see if you look them up. I do not know how they do it. I guess there is something about love which enables us to see the broken and wounded and do whatever we can to help end the pain.

His compassion rests on all His creation,[6] and He never wanted His creatures to be mistreated or to suffer. Sometimes animals need our help. Sometimes they are injured, lost, displaced, orphaned, or abused. Thank you to all of those people who help these animals even when it is inconvenient or makes others upset. Thank you also to those who extract animals from buildings, trees, and similar situations, but have compassion on them, as they do not understand they are not supposed to be there. I think sometimes we forget many animals are displaced because of us humans, whether it is from clearing land, building, developments such as roads, or us depleting animal food resources for our food and beauty products.

163

Thank you for whatever capacity you work in to help, for using whatever gift and ability He has given you. We could not do it without each other; it is too big. Please do not ever think what you do is not valuable, even if you are an individual who cleans, answers phones, does paperwork, volunteers, donates, or raises awareness. It is extremely valuable, even if it helps just one of His creatures. Father helped me realize He would stop the suffering even if only for one. That "one" is still His.

I have been trying to figure out exactly what my role is with animals, and perhaps He hasn't revealed it all to me yet; but I do think that, no matter what it is, education is key. Isn't the best way to protect someone to teach them the way? Didn't someone teach us about Jesus? Isn't the book of Proverbs all about teaching us? Doesn't the Holy Spirit teach us all things?[7] Father tells us the Way to protect us. For those of us now employed by Father, our mission is to go out and teach others about Jesus, preaching the gospel to all creation,[8] showing love to all.[9] Our gifts, abilities and work may look different, but the mission is still the same: to show all creation *Him*. We are His building,[10] field,[11] and weapons for righteousness.[12] For those of us who help animals, teaching animal care and stewardship is crucial but will only go so far. See, if the kind acts of the wicked are still cruel,[13] then we have to teach and show Jesus to them, because He is what changes the hearts and causes a righteous man to care for his animals.[14] In teaching and showing Him, we can help make lasting change and a difference for however long this earth has left, whether it is five years or two thousand years. This is true for any work His people are given to do. If Jesus is in it, He can change it.

You know, going back to the education part, I wish everyone knew that it is not good to feed wildlife bread, especially the ducks and geese. Those ducks and geese who consistently eat bread end up having nutritional deficiencies that can cause deformities and even death.[15] Or how migratory birds like songbirds and birds of prey (hawks, owls, eagles, etc.), are federally protected.[16] It is illegal to mess with their nests, or take a songbird or bird of prey into your possession unless you take them to a wildlife facility that has federal permits to rehab songbirds or birds of prey. Or how the best thing to do when you find wildlife who needs help, including baby wildlife who may need help, is to contact a wildlife facility ASAP. A lot of baby wildlife taken in by people who want to help and do good, end up being fed inappropriately (most baby wildlife cannot have cow's milk, for example), and it causes problems. Or the babies end up being aspirated (fluid in their lungs), when people try to give them liquids. This is especially true of birds, because they have a hole at the back of their tongue called a glottis which leads to the trachea.[17] When they are given water by someone who does not know this, they can accidently put the water right into the lungs. So, when wildlife needs help, it is best to contact a wildlife facility or a permitted facility for songbirds and birds of prey.

Anyway, thank you for what you do. I pray for the strength and energy to work those long days caring for these creatures. For the emotional support to see what you see and the hard decisions you have to make. Also, I pray for all of us to remember to add Jesus to the conversation wherever we can, because He can change the hearts of men[18] throughout all generations.

--Kristen

P.S. Does anyone else ever think about the new earth and wonder if we will be able to walk with the elephants, pet the lions, or play with all the birds?

CHAPTER 38

Those Unsure of Jesus

Luke 12:23 For life is more than food, and the body more than clothing.

John 1:10 (CSB) He was in the world, and the world was created through him, and yet the world did not recognize him.

1 Peter 3:18 For Christ also died for sins once for all, *the* just for *the* unjust, so that He might bring us to God, having been put to death in the flesh, but made alive in the spirit;

John 3:16 "For God so loved the world, that He gave His only begotten Son, that whoever believes in Him shall not perish, but have eternal life.

Matthew 22:8-10 (CSB) "Then he told his servants, 'The banquet is ready, but those who were invited were not worthy. Go then to where the roads exit the city and invite everyone you find to the banquet.' So those servants went out on the roads and gathered everyone they found, both evil and good. The wedding banquet was filled with guests.

Those Unsure of Jesus

Friend,

It is hard to know what to believe in this world, when everyone around us is telling us what to do and what to believe. There are so many opinions, options, religions, trends, and everyone has their stance on them all. No matter what everyone is telling each other, we can all agree this life is short. Do you ever wonder about this? I mean, life just flies by, especially as we get older. Our elders try to tell us that time flies and, before you know it, the years are gone, and you are not sure where they went. It is crazy how true this is.

Do you ever wonder if there is more to life, or if there is something after this life? What if all life is, is to be born, work to survive, retire, and die? After all the learning, graduations, games played, ladders climbed, milestones reached and places seen, what now, death? This life sounds sad. Could there be something better than this?

Do you ever wonder about this name, Jesus, so many people talk about? How His name has been around for over two thousand years? The Name[1] that generates so much anger yet so much happiness, the Name some people try to ban, and some people give praise and glory to? Maybe He could be real since all of this is happening?

You have probably figured out by now in this book that I believe He is real. I also hope with this book, that you can see the reason for my hope in Him.[2] My goal is not to convince you He is real, but yet He loves you,[3] and specifically you, the one reading this right now: *you*. For you to know there is hope and a better life. The world does not represent Jesus well, because they do not know Him.[4] Sometimes even we who believe and follow Him do not represent Him well, either. This is because we are not perfect and do not have the ability to be, but we can show you Him-- the One who Is.[5] There are some great books out there that people have written to help us see He is real. However, there is One greater, the number one bestselling book in all the world, and it is the Bible. God says it is living and active, reaching down to your marrow.[6] It definitely has shown this to be true for me. It will speak to you in crazy ways, even personal ways, if you let it, by reading it. I know this sounds weird, but those of us who have started to read it have come to know this to be true.

The words in the Bible are an account of how He loves us and how He loves *you*.[7] In summary, God created everything[8] and even took a moment to create you.[9] His Word says He gave you His own breath.[10] Sin entered the world because the enemy, Satan, deceived us and we did something God asked us not to do.[11] Because we did this, it changed how the relationship between creation worked[12] and separated us from God.[13] So, He sent us help by sending His Son Jesus from Heaven,[14] who is God manifested into flesh like us.[15] Jesus took on our punishment for our wrongs by dying the death we should have died, because we all have sinned.[16] This was a gift to us,[17] because He loves us.[18] He rose from the dead after three days,[19] showing us, He overcomes all and even death cannot stop Him.[20] Because of this, if we turn from our wrongs, repent, and accept His gift, we are then made part of His family,[21] made right because of Jesus.[22] This is our salvation, because Jesus is the *only* way out of Hell into Heaven.[23]

After Jesus rose and appeared to many,[24] He then went back to be with God and sent His Spirit here to earth to help us,[25] because He loves us. The Bible, which is prophetic,[26] tells us Jesus will come again[27] and gather those of us who have been made righteous because of Him.[28] Oh, and the enemy who deceived us --Jesus will defeat him.[29]

See the whole account is about how He loves us and how He loves *you*. Whether you believe it is a real account or not, there is a gentle[30] but mighty[31] Being who cares for and loves you, my friend. All of us who know Him know this. This is why we take the time and try to show you Him. He cares about all His creation and cares about you.[32] His eyes saw you before you had a form, and your days were written and planned before the day you were born.[33] He formed you[34] and gave you His breath[35] so you could be alive on this earth today. How special you are for God, the only God,[36] to share His breath with you. You being alive on this earth wasn't something that He had no say in.

You were fearfully and wonderfully created[37] no matter what anyone tells you. If you were the only one on the earth, Jesus still would have come for you and died just for you, because He tells us He goes after the one.[38] He tells us He is always with us[39] and wants everyone to be saved. He does not want anyone to die and not have eternal life.[40] There is hope and a better life than to be born, work to survive, retire, and die, because He loves you. Life continues after this life and Jesus wants you to have eternal life with Him and not in Hell. He truly wants the best for you. Choose Him. Live for Him.

Friend, please know God set aside a moment just for you--to create you. He specifically loves you, died for you, searches for you, and He is waiting for that moment, for you to believe in Him.

Jesus loves you, friend. You have been invited to the banquet.[41]

--Kristen

P.S. Romans 10:9 "If you confess with your mouth, "Jesus is Lord," and believe in your heart that God raised him from the dead, you will be saved."

BONUS

CHAPTER 39

Summary of the Bible

1 John 4:7-8 Beloved, let us love one another, for love is from God; and everyone who loves is born of God and knows God. The one who does not love does not know God, for God is love.

John 3:16 "For God so loved the world, that He gave His only begotten Son, that whoever believes in Him shall not perish, but have eternal life.

Matthew 22:36-39 "Teacher, which is the great commandment in the Law?" And He said to him, " 'YOU SHALL LOVE THE LORD YOUR GOD WITH ALL YOUR HEART, AND WITH ALL YOUR SOUL, AND WITH ALL YOUR MIND.' This is the great and foremost commandment. The second is like it, 'YOU SHALL LOVE YOUR NEIGHBOR AS YOURSELF.'

Romans 8:38-39 For I am convinced that neither death, nor life, nor angels, nor principalities, nor things present, nor things to come, nor powers, nor height, nor depth, nor any other created thing, will be able to separate us from the love of God, which is in Christ Jesus our Lord.

1 Corinthians 13:1-8 If I speak with the tongues of men and of angels, but do not have love, I have become a noisy gong or a clanging cymbal. If I have *the gift of* prophecy, and know all mysteries and all knowledge; and if I have all faith, so as to remove mountains, but do not have love, I am nothing. And if I give all my possessions to feed *the poor,* and if I surrender my body to be burned, but do not have love, it profits me nothing. Love is patient, love is kind *and* is not jealous; love does not brag *and* is not arrogant, does not act unbecomingly; it does not seek its own, is not provoked, does not take into account a wrong *suffered,* does not rejoice in unrighteousness, but rejoices with the truth; bears all things, believes all things, hopes all things, endures all things. Love never fails; but if *there are gifts of* prophecy, they will be done away; if *there are* tongues, they will cease; if *there is* knowledge, it will be done away.

Summary of the Bible

Love.

CHAPTER 40

The Two Lines

Matthew 7:13-14 "Enter through the narrow gate; for the gate is wide and the way is broad that leads to destruction, and there are many who enter through it. For the gate is small and the way is narrow that leads to life, and there are few who find it.

Proverbs 14:12 There is a way *which seems* right to a man, but its end is the way of death.

1 Corinthians 1:18 For the word of the cross is foolishness to those who are perishing, but to us who are being saved it is the power of God.

Matthew 13:40-43 So just as the tares are gathered up and burned with fire, so shall it be at the end of the age. The Son of Man will send forth His angels, and they will gather out of His kingdom all stumbling blocks, and those who commit lawlessness, and will throw them into the furnace of fire; in that place there will be weeping and gnashing of teeth. Then THE RIGHTEOUS WILL SHINE FORTH AS THE SUN in the kingdom of their Father. He who has ears, let him hear.

1 John 5:11-13 And the testimony is this, that God has given us eternal life, and this life is in His Son. He who has the Son has the life; he who does not have the Son of God does not have the life. *This Is Written That You May Know* these things I have written to you who believe in the name of the Son of God, so that you may know that you have eternal life.

The Two Lines

It's one of those days today where the sun is out, and the temperature is just right. As I walk down the road, a pleasant breeze gently touches my face. I see the trees sway and hear the birds sing as they forage about. I always have wondered what they are singing about. I wonder if they are ever trying to tell us something. It would be neat to know but, even if not, it is nice to hear their songs as I walk down this road to the line. I guess I could say, the life around me with the trees and birds, brings some sort of comfort to me, like a peace I can't explain.[1]

As I make my way to the line that the world has been telling us to go stand in, I cannot help but wonder what is at the end of the line. All I have been told is everything I need and want will be given to me and to just go stand in the line. They made it easy to find the line as the path was wide and paved.[2]

I must be getting close; I can see a large crowd in the distance.

After some time, I finally make it to the gate to enter the line. There are a lot of people in this line and, before too long, many will be behind me as I see them traveling this way. Everyone is talking amongst themselves or quietly standing by, like me. Every once in a while, as the line moves slowly ahead, I catch a clip of a conversation. One in particular has my attention. An individual asked another why they were standing in this line, and the response that followed was, "Because everyone else is; it just seems right."[3] This has taken hold of my thoughts, because I did not think we had a choice. No one talked about any other option.

The line has moved up enough for me to see what is out ahead. There is a ship. It is a really big and dark battle looking ship, and everyone in this line is boarding it. I wonder where it is going.

Some more time passes and, as the line draws closer to the ship, it seems to be that the environment around me is changing. In fact, I do not hear the birds anymore. As I look around trying to see where the birds went, I catch a glimpse of a few people in the distance to the right. They are outside of the line that is fenced in and seem to be in some sort of distress. I wonder if they are trying to get into the line.

With every step it is starting to sound like people screaming. It appears the people in my line are angry with the ones outside of the line. I guess they do not want the ones on the outside to cut in line. The more I watch them, the more intrigued I am to know what they are saying.

I finally speak out loud the question in my mind, "Who are those people outside of the line?" Hoping someone around me will know the answer.

A man standing a few people in front of me turns around and answers, "They call themselves fishers of men."[4] Another one turns around and laughs saying, "They give this whole speech about how Jesus is our help[5] and will provide us with everything we need,[6] to come join them in their line. How foolish they are,"[7] As he turns back around, he adds, "Jesus can't help us."

I am confused by their answers, as I thought these people wanted in our line, not trying to get people out of our line... Wait, so there is another choice besides this line, and these people are choosing *not* to stand in it even though everyone else is? Hmm...oh, and Jesus--I have heard of Him. He is that Guy who died on a cross to save someone.[8] Wait...to save someone from what?

The unrest in the people in my line is increasing. They are screaming at the ones in the other line, calling them names, mocking them,[9] wishing for them to die. Yet the ones on the outside are responding differently with kindness and compassion,[10] urging us that this ship is not what we think, and Jesus is the only way.

I can't stop wondering and watching these people pleading their case. Why would they keep doing so and being so kind after all the violence towards them? Is there something they know that we don't? What would make them continue, and why are the people in my line so angry? Are they mad at what they are saying? What is so foolish about a Man saving someone?

These people set apart[11] on the outside do seem crazy. There is no ship or anything over there, just them. On the other hand, I cannot help wondering why there is this unsettled feeling inside of me. My eyes glance from side to side to see if there might be anyone else feeling it too.

As I am looking around, a woman on the outside comes close to where I'm standing. I am taken aback by the compassion and sincerity in her eyes. She begs us to listen to her. I listen as she proclaims, "The kingdom of Heaven is near.[12] Our ways may seem right to us,[13] but Jesus is the only way.[14] Please, if you have ears to hear[15] please listen to us. Jesus died for our sins and rose again.[16] He will come back.[17] Confess with your mouth that Jesus is Lord and believe in your heart that God raised Him from the dead and you will be saved."[18] There it is again, being saved, but saved *from* what?

I hear another one on the outside say, "Even the birds know."[19] The birds, yes, wait even the birds know? The birds know what, that Jesus saves?

There are a few people left in front of me before it will be my turn to board. As I wait, all I can hear is one of the fishers of men saying over and over, "Jesus can save you". I still do not know what He is saving everyone from, but it must not be good if we need to be saved from it... right? As I contemplate this and step closer and closer to the ship, I realize no one else is paying any attention to the few on the outside anymore, so maybe I shouldn't either.

It is my turn to board the ship, and I step up to where the guard is directing everyone in. I go to take a step onto the ship, and I hear behind me the same man on the outside with a soft sorrowful voice say, "Please". It is as if he knows I am listening to him... I pause while the guard at the door stares at me with vexation, and I listen to the man urgently speaking to me, "Jesus can save you". The guard becomes violent with me, and commands me to get on the ship. Appalled, I look up at him and say "No!" Immediately, I turn and climb over the fence and walk over to the few on the outside. I am met with embrace and love-- nothing I have experienced before. After a moment of this, I notice the sound of a bird again.

I'm not exactly sure what made me turn around and join these people, but the unsettled feeling is gone. I watch as the ship loads up the last of those in the line and starts to take its course. As it turns and goes about, I stand perplexed staring at the name on the back of the ship. It reads: DEATH.[20] One of the fishers of men notices me observing DEATH sailing away and tells me with a comforting voice, "Don't worry, the storm is almost over and our Help is on the way."[21] With an astonished face and a tearful voice, I ask him, "What is the name of our ship?" He smiles and says, "Redeemer."[22]

CHAPTER 41

Epic God

Revelation 3:14 (CSB) "Write to the angel of the church in Laodicea: Thus says the Amen, the faithful and true witness, the originator of God's creation:

Revelation 1:17-18 When I saw Him, I fell at His feet like a dead man. And He placed His right hand on me, saying, "Do not be afraid; I am the first and the last, and the living One; and I was dead, and behold, I am alive forever-more, and I have the keys of death and of Hades.

Romans 13:11-12 (CSB) Besides this, since you know the time, it is already the hour for you to wake up from sleep, because now our salvation is nearer than when we first believed. The night is nearly over, and the day is near; so let us discard the deeds of darkness and put on the armor of light.

Exodus 15:3 (HCSB) The Lord is a warrior; Yahweh is His name.

Revelation 17:14 These will wage war against the Lamb, and the Lamb will overcome them, because He is Lord of lords and King of kings, and those who are with Him *are the* called and chosen and faithful."

Epic God

A long time ago in a galaxy far, far away, and right here, right now, in this galaxy too, there was and is a good Guy who has been since the beginning, and His name is God.[1] He is not a lone ranger though, because along with Him there are two other good guys[2] through which all exist and move about, and nothing would be without them.[3] They are the fantastic 3. They are enthroned above the earth,[4] and the sky proclaims Their majesty,[5] They named all the stars,[6] are not served by human hands, and give life and breath and all things.[7] They can be everywhere all at the same time,[8] the past, *Back to the Future*, infinity plus beyond, and can transform into anything. See nothing is impossible[9] for the One who created everything.[10]

Now there is a bad guy too. He was a murderer from the beginning.[11] He tried to say he was the father, but he is not, except the father of lies.[12] He *is* the enemy, masquerading as an ally.[13] World, *we have a problem here*, because the serpent deceived and humans believed.[14] So, a person came along *who defies the odds, who defies logic*, and does it all without boxing.[15] This man is a super man. He is man and God[16] at the same time, and he does not change[17] no matter how much the world may be. He is Christ, Jesus Christ,[18] the true bond,[19] God the Father,[20] the great I Am,[21] number 1,[22] Kong's King, the only King the jungle has ever seen, He is Captain of America and beyond, *King of the world*, and the true Guardian of all the galaxies.[23] He came here from the Three,[24] to fight the forces of evil and all that is unseen.[25] Kind of like *Ghostbusters*, except without the Psychomagnotheric Slime everywhere, you know the slimy stuff that is green. He does not *need* a shield, or a weapon, because He *Is*.[26] He only needs to speak.[27] His words penetrate deep into a human's soul, spirit, joints, and marrow.[28] He also does not need big green muscles, claws, a web, laser, or wand, because His Spirit's Sword is stronger and sharper than any of these combined.[29] He does not need an Invisible Boatmobile, Batmobile, motorcycle, Turtle Van, or Starship to fight evil schemes. Because He flies on the wings of the wind[30] swooping down like an eagle,[31] His voice flashes flames of fire,[32] a consuming fire,[33] trampling His enemies,[34] all that is evil. He rains down sulfur,[35] sends scorching winds on the wicked,[36] inflicts confusion,[37] making enemy turn against enemy[38]. He will even pronounce judgements; see where Jeremiah says woe to us, we are ruined?[39]

He went to the cross for all who would believe, to take our punishment so we would not have to bleed.[40] It is an offer you shouldn't refuse,[41] because He can take your dead body and make it living,[42] no more smelling like a zombie. Death could not stop Him,[43] impossible mission it seemed, as He took His last breath hanging from the tree.[44] But, He was just getting the keys of death and Hades.[45] You see, not only is He the firstborn from the dead,[46] He is a *Tomb Raider,* saving those just like He said.[47] Have you read the book by the Originator?[48] He is a pretty cool dude. He was the first one to say, *I'll be back,* and the second one, too.[49] He rose from the grave and will come again.[50] He said if you are not with Him, you are against Him.[51] Being for Him is better; all you have to do is take a breath, confess with your mouth that Jesus is Lord, and believe in your heart God raised Him from the dead.[52] Then try your best to do what He says, it truly is for your good, health to your bones,[53] and a crown of beauty on your head.[54] So then, when you are not behind the enemy's line, you do not have to worry. He makes your heart brave.[55] And He will show you His faithful love,[56] kindness,[57] compassion,[58] and grace.[59] He provides clothes for you even when you mess up and eat the fruit,[60] and gives you a warning and a plan to build a boat when a flood is coming soon.[61] He allows you to have babies,[62] puts you in palaces next to kings,[63] sends plagues for your release,[64] provides in the wilderness,[65] and parts the seas.[66] He keeps you safe in fires even when it is turned up seven times more than customary,[67] keeps you safe from or gives you the ability to fight lions and giants as you are walking down the street,[68] in a lion's den,[69] or when you are just trying to take your brothers something to eat.[70] He sends His angels to protect you in all your ways[71] and will keep giving you new mercies every single day.[72] He will save you with a big fish[73] *In the Heart of the Sea,* heal your wounds, sickness, and disease,[74] and allow you to catch all the fish you can eat.[75] He gives you His Spirit, so you can *phone home,* and will teach you all you need to know.[76] And when times get hard, He will even give you supernatural ability to keep swimming.[77] He will remove all of your chains,[78] and when you tell others how He saved you from the dark, it will cause a chain of reaction of healing broken hearts.[79] Hmm what's that song? *Way maker, miracle worker*[80]...

You are His precious, a treasured one of the King.[81] In the end, after this earth, He will also take you to be with Him, in a whole new world,[82] the land of the living, where no one is lost, the greatest place to be. Who was it that said, *there's no place like home*? Wasn't it Dorothy?

Don't you see we are all being recruited?[83] The night is nearly over, and the daylight is near[84]; a time where the team of good and evil will battle[85]; a time for some of dread and fear.[86] Would you rather be on the team of defeat or the team of victory? Joel 3:9 says "Proclaim this among the nations: Prepare for holy war; rouse the warriors; let all the men of war advance and attack!" You see, it will not just be a mortal combat, in the end it will be a holy war. In Matthew, Jesus said He came to bring a sword.[87]

He is a warrior and Yahweh is His name,[88] the only One who is mighty to save.[89] The enemy has no power over Him[90]; do not be deceived by his imitation games. Know there is more than *300* with Yahweh, countless thousands plus thousands of thousands surround Him saying worthy is the Lamb, all day every day.[91]

So, on that day when the sky opens[92] and He roars,[93] Heaven and earth will shake,[94] even *Godzilla* will tremble as he runs away. If you think you need a bigger boat to escape Him, I do not think this will do, because the winds and waves obey Him[95] and even the *Jaws* of Leviathan too.[96] He Himself said no creature is hidden from Him and must give an account.[97] His eyes are everywhere keeping watch on the wicked and the good,[98] no one is left out. David said in Psalm 139:7-10 "Where can I go to escape your Spirit? Where can I flee from your presence? If I go up to heaven, you are there; if I make my bed in Sheol, you are there. If I fly on the wings of the dawn and settle down on the western horizon, even there your hand will lead me; your right hand will hold on to me." So, there is no escaping Him, it doesn't matter what you do. In fact, if He decided to withdraw His breath, all would perish and return to the dust once again, too.[99]

Before the day comes, turn your hearts to Him and let Him rescue you. Isaiah 45:22-25 says "Turn to me and be saved, all the ends of the earth. For I am God, and there is no other. By myself I have sworn; truth has gone from my mouth, a word that will not be revoked: Every knee will bow to me, every tongue will swear allegiance. It will be said about me, 'Righteousness and strength are found only in the Lord.' " All who are enraged against him will come to him and be put to shame. All the descendants of Israel will be justified and boast in the Lord."

In the end there will be no suspense, just like in most movies the good Guy will win. He told us He would, you can read it in Revelation.[100] So why is the enemy trying to deceive and recruit? I am not so sure, because the Word says it is the great day of the Lord,[101] not of the liar.

Jesus, the greatest hero there can be, He and His army of horses and angels are the real *Justice League*.[102] They will defeat the dragon and throw him into the fire because of who all he deceived.[103] Those who are against Jesus will pay the penalty of eternal destruction[104]; Love they will no longer see, which will be uncomfortable as Hell for all eternity.[105] But all those who heard His voice will be avenged[106] and, along with all creation, we will praise Him.[107] All blessing, honor, glory, dominion to the One on the throne and to the Lamb.[108] He is the Alpha and Omega, Beginning and End.[109] All His praise will be said by every nation, tribe, people, and language, the sound of a great multitude.[110] So, like Solomon says, the conclusion of the matter is to fear God[111]... may the good force be with you.

CHAPTER 42

Those Enduring to the End

1 John 5:19 We know that we are of God, and that the whole world lies in *the power of* the evil one.

John 15:18-19 "If the world hates you, you know that it has hated Me before *it hated* you. If you were of the world, the world would love its own; but because you are not of the world, but I chose you out of the world, because of this the world hates you.

Revelation 3:11 I am coming quickly; hold fast what you have, so that no one will take your crown.

Isaiah 5:20 Woe to those who call evil good, and good evil; who substitute darkness for light and light for darkness; who substitute bitter for sweet and sweet for bitter!

Matthew 24:12-13 Because lawlessness is increased, most people's love will grow cold. But the one who endures to the end, he will be saved.

Those Enduring to the End

Life on this earth is a battle. Every second of every moment. It started in Genesis 3.

The world is in the sway of the enemy.[1] The enemy is a liar.[2] Perhaps the world has been lying.

The Bible says all nations will be deceived.[3] Lie after lie, nations still believe. They think the world is a lifeguard but can't see they are only drowning.

Every effort to steal, kill, and destroy[4] the truth is made. If Jesus is the truth,[5] then it makes sense why anything to do with Him, they want to do away.

Those enduring know Who the world hates,[6] but they will stand firm because of Who they love.[7]

The road is narrow for the eyes that see and ears that hear.[8] This is why when the masses line up, those enduring have to remember to pause and think through to make sure destruction isn't near.[9]

They ask for wisdom that God generously gives,[10] because it is hard to tell what is true when the serpent is as cunning as it gets.[11]

Some enduring might think from time to time, "If we all have the same Spirit in us,[12] then how, how all the division, how all of the complete opposite thoughts of minds? How can it be some say yes, some say ehh, some say never? What is going on?"

Those enduring see it getting darker and darker out there as the days go by and wonder if this is part of the oil in the lamps that will run dry.[13]

It has become increasingly clear they are not of this current world[14] as they see right and wrong switched thinking, "What movie is this?" But they know it really is just a three-hour tour, and that the time is near.[15] Some even hear the tick tocking, as they see how the world is distracting people year after year.

The banquet is coming soon.[16] For those who have pledged their allegiance with the true God, the eternal King,[17] they will be dressed in the right clothing.[18]

When the end comes, Jesus says it will be time to rest.[19] But for now, they have to stand firm steadying their ship, not giving up their crown for anything no matter how much time is left.[20]

To not be deceived—seek Jesus, pray, fast, and praise; those enduring know this is the only way.

Those enduring must know, no matter how much the world says they are alone, there are many more enduring all over the world, standing with one another on the   Cornerstone.[21]

May Jesus squeeze their hand, so they can know He is still holding on to them.

Those enduring know, no matter what they see or hear, nothing is worth giving up eternity. They can't give up their crown for something that will be destroyed; instead they hold on and give up this world for what will remain.[22]

So, when the world is against them, those enduring take a deep breath and remember forever is on the other side of this thing.[23] It will be okay. Nothing can hurt you again. Life is on the other side. Remember: He has the keys;[24] you will not be forsaken.[25]

Once on the other side, the ones who endured will see all of the others who also fought and held onto Truth. They might even say to each other, "Man that was something--what we all just went through!"

Let it be said that we stood firm for Him when He reads our name in that book which belongs to the Lamb.[26]

Steady the ship of your mind on things above. Arch that bow in your heart to hold on to Truth. Take hold of that Hand that has always been holding on to you. Because of that Hand, we don't lose.[27]

Jesus Christ is King.[28]

Endure to the end.[29]

Notes

All verse references in Notes are from the Christian Standard Bible (CSB), unless noted otherwise.

Dedication
1. See Jeremiah 10:6
2. Attr. Singh, S. Sundar. "I Have Decided to Follow Jesus".
   Mid 1800's.
3. See Revelation 5:13

Greetings
1. See Job 7:7 (NASB)
2. See Philippians 4:5, Psalm 145:18
3. See Hebrews 13:5
4. See Hebrews 11:1
5. See Lamentations 3:22-23
6. See Genesis 8:11
7. See Hebrews 10:24-25
8. See Deuteronomy 6:3, Revelation 21:1-4 (NASB)

Chapter 1: The Book
1. See Hebrews 11:1
2. See Lamentations 3:22-23
3. See 1 Samuel 17:42-45
4. See Matthew 13:25 *while this verse in the parable is speaking on the kingdom of Heaven, it also reminds me of how the enemy can sneak in and try to diminish our hope with lies.*
5. Hebrews 4:12 (NASB), Ephesians 6:17, Revelation 1:16
6. See John 3:8

Chapter 2: You
1. See Genesis 1:1, Acts 17:24, John 1:3
2. See Isaiah 45:5
3. See Psalm 100:3
4. See Isaiah 64:8, Hebrews 12:9 (NASB)
5. See Matthew 5:48
6. See Proverbs 30:5
7. See Revelation 15:3
8. See Psalm 24:8
9. See Psalm 46:7
10. See Job 7:20
11. See Exodus 3:6
12. See Deuteronomy 32:4
13. See Genesis 49:24
14. See Isaiah 41:17
15. See 1 John 4:16

16. See 2 Peter 3:9
17. See Romans 2:4, Psalm 86:5
18. See 1 Corinthians 13:4-5 (HCSB)
19. See Jeremiah 31:34, Isaiah 43:25
20. See Psalm 5:4
21. See Proverbs 12:22
22. See 1 Corinthians 13:7 (HCSB)
23. See Psalm 102:25-27
24. See Psalm 119:68
25. See 2 Thessalonians 3:3
26. See James 3:17, Matthew 21:5
27. See Matthew 11:29 (NASB)
28. See Nehemiah 9:17
29. See Psalm 116:5
30. See Psalm 103:8
31. See Psalm 86:15
32. See Luke 6:36
33. See John 17:25
34. See Psalm 147:5
35. See Deuteronomy 10:17
36. See Deuteronomy 7:21
37. See Nehemiah 9:32
38. See Ephesians 1:17
39. See 1 John 1:5
40. See Deuteronomy 4:24
41. See Exodus 34:14
42. See Nahum 1:2
43. See Jeremiah 50:34
44. See Job 9:4, Romans 16:27
45. See 1 John 3:20
46. See Job 9:4
47. See Nahum 1:3
48. See Jeremiah 23:23-24 (NASB)
49. See Job 23:13
50. See Proverbs 30:5
51. See 1 Kings 19:12
52. See 1 Peter 5:10
53. See Psalm 147:3
54. See Romans 15:5
55. See Romans 15:5
56. See Romans 15:13 (NASB)
57. See Romans 16:20
58. See Psalm 31:5
59. See 1 Peter 5:10
60. See 2 Corinthians 1:3
61. See 2 Corinthians 1:3

62. See Isaiah 43:3
63. See Isaiah 47:4
64. See Psalm 33:5
65. See Isaiah 61:8
66. See Psalm 37:28
67. See Job 13:3
68. See Hebrews 1:3, Hebrews 8:1
69. See 2 Peter 1:17
70. See Job 6:10
71. See 1 Samuel 15:29
72. See Genesis 21:33
73. See Revelation 1:8
74. See Exodus 3:14
75. See John 4:24
76. See Genesis 1:26
77. See 2 Corinthians 3:18
78. See 2 Corinthians 3:18
79. See Philippians 2:7 (HCSB)
80. See Numbers 6:25
81. See 2 Chronicles 16:9
82. See Zechariah 2:8
83. See Psalm 34:15
84. See Isaiah 40:5
85. See Psalm 18:15
86. See 1 Kings 9:3
87. See Psalm 89:13
88. See Jeremiah 1:9
89. See Exodus 33:23
90. See Psalm 18:9
91. See Exodus 3:2-4
92. See Exodus 16:10, Exodus 13:21
93. See Exodus 24:17, Exodus 13:21
94. See Psalm 91:4
95. See Deuteronomy 32:11
96. See Daniel 7:9-10
97. See 1 Timothy 1:17
98. See John 1:18
99. See John 6:46, John 1:18
100. See Psalm 11:7
101. See Matthew 18:10
102. See Philippians 4:19
103. See Job 26:14
104. See Psalm 138:8, Proverbs 16:4
105. See Romans 5:8
106. See 1 Peter 5:7
107. See Daniel 4:3
108. See John 15:15

109. See John 3:16, Matthew 7:11
110. See Isaiah 51:12
111. See James 4:12
112. See Isaiah 42:16
113. See Romans 10:13
114. See Psalm 121:5
115. See Job 33:29-30
116. See Deuteronomy 3:22
117. See Ezekiel 34:16, Luke 19:10
118. See Psalm 94:10
119. See Acts 17:25, 1 Timothy 6:17, Philippians 4:19
120. See Matthew 18:12-14
121. See Psalm 103:4
122. See Matthew 23:22
123. See Amos 9:1
124. See Genesis 3:8
125. See 2 Samuel 22:11
126. See Genesis 1:2, Deuteronomy 32:11
127. See Ezekiel 21:31
128. See Revelation 1:16
129. See Acts 4:24 (HCSB), Genesis 16:13 (HCSB)
130. See 1 John 5:20 (HCSB)
131. See Daniel 7:9
132. See Jeremiah 10:6
133. See Romans 16:27
134. See Psalm 78:35, Psalm 83:18 (HCSB)
135. See 1 Timothy 1:17 (NASB)
136. See Hebrews 10:31, Jeremiah 10:10
137. See Psalm 83:18 (HCSB)
138. See Amos 9:6
139. See Exodus 3:14

Chapter 3: The Name
1. See John 10:30, John 1:18
2. See 2 Corinthians 13:13, Matthew 28:19, John 15:26, John 1:18, Galatians 4:6, Genesis 1:26, 1 Corinthians 2:12
3. See Matthew 12:50
4. See 1 Peter 2:24
5. See Ephesians 2:4-9
6. See Mark 2:15
7. See John 7:28-29
8. See John 13:21
9. See Matthew 26:34
10. See Matthew 27:30
11. See John 19:3
12. See Mark 15:16-20 (HCSB)
13. See Genesis 2:9

14. See Acts 2:22-23
15. See John 3:16, John 15:13, Romans 5:8
16. See Revelation 1:5, 2 Timothy 4:18
17. See Psalm 40:2
18. See Psalm 34:18
19. See Matthew 18:12, Matthew 28:19-20
20. See Matthew 19:26
21. See Luke 22:49-51
22. See Deuteronomy 32:39, John 4:26
23. See 1 Peter 2:25
24. See 1 Peter 5:4
25. See John 1:29
26. See Philippians 2:5-7
27. See John 1:1, John 1:14, Revelation 19:13
28. See John 18:12, John 1:9-10
29. See Galatians 3:19
30. See John 15:1
31. See Zechariah 3:8, Zechariah 6:12, Jeremiah 23:5
32. See John 6:35
33. See John 14:6
34. See Revelation 22:16
35. See Isaiah 9:6
36. See Revelation 17:14
37. See John 11:25
38. See Zechariah 9:9
39. See Acts 3:14
40. See Ephesians 1:6, Matthew 3:17
41. See Revelation 3:14
42. See 1 Corinthians 2:8
43. See Revelation 22:13
44. See 3 John 1:7
45. See John 20:31
46. See John 14:6
47. See John 10:9
48. See 1 Chronicles 29:11
49. See Matthew 16:15-16

Chapter 4: Greater Are You
1. See 1 Corinthians 2:12, Galatians 4:6
2. See 1 Thessalonians 4:8
3. See Romans 1:4
4. See 1 Peter 4:14
5. See John 14:17
6. See Hebrews 10:29
7. See Isaiah 11:2
8. See Acts 1:8, 1 Thessalonians 1:5
9. See John 15:26

10. See Nehemiah 9:20
11. See Galatians 3:14
12. See Hebrews 9:14
13. See John 6:63
14. See Ephesians 1:13
15. See Ephesians 1:14, 2 Corinthians 1:22
16. See John 7:38-39 (NASB)
17. See Galatians 4:6
18. See John 14:2-3
19. See 1 Corinthians 1:7
20. See James 4:8
21. See Ephesians 6:17, Hebrews 4:12 (NASB)
22. See Job 33:4 (NASB)
23. See Job 33:4 (NASB)
24. See Psalm 139:7-10
25. See Isaiah 40:28, Colossians 1:15-17
26. See Matthew 28:18
27. See John 6:69
28. See Matthew 5:48
29. See Revelation 4:8
30. See 1 Timothy 1:17
31. See Romans 8:9-11, 1 Corinthians 3:16 (NASB)
32. See 1 Corinthians 3:16 (NASB)
33. See 1 Corinthians 2:13, 1 John 2:27
34. See Matthew 10:19-20, 2 Samuel 23:2
35. See Ephesians 3:16
36. See John 16:8-11
37. See John 14:26
38. See 1 Corinthians 2:10
39. See Galatians 5:18
40. See John 16:13
41. See John 14:26
42. See Romans 8:16
43. See 2 Corinthians 1:3-4
44. See John 3:8
45. See Acts 2:38
46. See Romans 8:26-27
47. See 1 Corinthians 12:4-11 (NASB)
48. See 2 Corinthians 3:17
49. See Psalm 145:9
50. See 1 Corinthians 3:16 (NASB)
51. See Galatians 5:22-23
52. See 1 John 4:4

Chapter 6: Thank You
1. See Ephesians 5:20
2. See 1 John 4:16

3. See Genesis 1:31
4. See Psalm 139:13
5. See Job 10:11
6. See Genesis 2:7
7. See Hebrews 4:12 (NASB)
8. Gillen, Dr. Alan L., and Jason Conrad. "Life Is in the Blood". Answers in Genesis, 2 August 2019, https://answersingenesis.org/biology/microbiology/life-is-in-the-blood/.
9. IBID
10. Brinson, Heather M. "Constantly Beating Death". Answers in Genesis, 1 October 2009, https://answersingenesis.org/human-body/heart/.
11. Paturi, Joseph. "God's Masterpiece". Answers in Genesis, 1 September 1998, https://answersingenesis.org/kids/anatomy/the-human-body/.
12. Demick, David. "The Breath of Life, God's Gift to All Creatures". Answers in Genesis, 1 December 2004, https://answersingenesis.org/human-body/the-breath-of-life/.
13. DeWitt, David A. "Shaped By Experiences". Answers in Genesis, 1 October 2009, https://answersingenesis.org/human-body/brain/brain-experiences/.
14. Savige, Craig. "Electrical design in the human body". Answers in Genesis, 1 December 1999, https://answersingenesis.org/evidence-for-creation/design-in-nature/electrical-design-in-the-human-body/.
15. "Spilling the Beans on Digestion: World Digestive Health Day". Answers in Genesis, 29 May 2019, https://answersingenesis.org/human-body/world-digestive-health-day/.
16. Gillen, Dr. Alan L., and Jason Conrad. "Our Impressive Immune System: More Than a Defense". Answers in Genesis, 15 January 2014, https://answersingenesis.org/human-body/our-impressive-immune-system-more-than-a-defense/.
17. Munoz, Kissairis. "7 Benefits of Fasting and the Best Types to Try for Better Health". Dr. Axe, 10 January 2018, https://draxe.com/nutrition/benefits-fasting/.
18. Littleton, Jeanette. "God's Gift of Sleep". Answers in Genesis, 1 March 2019, https://answersingenesis.org/human-body/brain/gods-gift-sleep/.
19. "CAN LAUGHTER INCREASE YOUR HEART HEALTH?" Cardiovascular Specialist of South Florida, https://southflcardio.com/can-laughter-increase-your-heart-health/.
20. Menton, Dr. David. "Bones, God's Living Girders". Answers in Genesis, 1 October 2009, https://answersingenesis.org/human-body/bones/.
21. Menton, Dr. David. "Facial Expressions—The Universal Language, Human Wonders". Answers in Genesis, 1 January 2015, https://answersingenesis.org/human-body/facial-expressions-universal-language/.
22. Menton, Dr. David. "The Seeing Eye". Answers in Genesis, 19 May 2008, https://answersingenesis.org/human-body/eyes/the-seeing-eye/.
23. Menton, Dr. David. "The Hearing Ear". Answers in Genesis, 29 August 2007, https://answersingenesis.org/human-body/the-hearing-ear/.

24. McIntosh, Prof. Andy. "The Wonder of the Human Voice". Answers in Genesis, 6 September 2019, https://answersingenesis.org/human-body/the-wonder-of-the-human-voice/.
25. See Romans 8:28
26. See Genesis 2:7
27. See Genesis 2:7
28. See Colossians 1:16, Genesis 2:19
29. See Genesis 1:6-7 (KJV), Genesis 1:14-18 (KJV)
30. Lisle, Dr. Jason. "Discoveries of Order in the Sun, Astronomy". Answers in Genesis, 1 April 2012, https://answersingenesis.org/astronomy/sun/new-discoveries-of-order-in-the-sun/.
31. Anderson, Dr. Ross. "Proportionally Perfect for Life: O2, CO2, N2, Formed to Be Inhabited". Answers in Genesis, 19 January 2018, https://answersingenesis.org/chemistry/proportionally-perfect-for-life/.
32. See Isaiah 55:10
33. See Genesis 27:28
34. See Psalm 84:3
35. Guaglione, Bob. "21 REASONS WHY I BELIEVE IN GOD: BEES". Calvary Chapel Delaware County, 9 January 2014, https://ccdelco.com/article/21-reasons-why-i-believe-in-god-bees/.
36. Johnson, James J. S. "Providential Planting". Answers in Genesis, 1 June 1997, https://answersingenesis.org/evidence-for-creation/providential-planting/.
37. See Genesis 2:9
38. See 1 Peter 2:24
39. See Jeremiah 8:7
40. See Luke 12:27-28
41. See Psalm 51:7, Song of Songs 4:13-14, Matthew 2:11
42. See Genesis 2:7
43. See 2 Corinthians 6:18
44. See John 15:12-15, Proverbs 3:32
45. See Isaiah 25:1
46. See 1 Peter 4:10
47. See 2 Peter 1:3
48. See Luke 12:29-31, Philippians 4:19
49. See Psalm 91:14
50. Proverbs 3:5-6 (KJV) Proverbs 16:9 (KJV)
51. See Psalm 100:3, Isaiah 43:1
52. See 1 Corinthians 11:12, Revelation 4:11
53. See Job 34:14-15

Chapter 7: What Place is This?
1. See Jeremiah 29:11
2. See Ezekiel 34:16
3. See Philippians 1:6

Chapter 8: The Plan
1. "How Do Birds Keep Warm in the Winter?" U.S. Fish and Wildlife Service, https://www.fws.gov/midwest/news/WinterWarmth.html.
2. "How Do Birds Cope With Cold in Winter." Audubon, https://www.audubon.org/how-do-birds-cope-cold-winter.
3. IBID
4. See Acts 17:24
5. See Proverbs 13:12
6. See Daniel 9:3
7. See Romans 8:26
8. See Psalm 56:8
9. See Jonah 4:6 (HCSB)

Chapter 9: Where Are You?
1. See Job 36:7
2. See Psalm 145:18
3. See Psalm 37:28, Hebrews 13:5, Matthew 28:20
4. See Mark 9:24
5. Spafford, Horatio G. "It Is Well with My Soul". 1873.
6. See Psalm 36:7, Psalm 91:4

Chapter 10: 7th Day
1. See Joshua 6:1-3
2. See Proverbs 18:10
3. See Joshua 6:4
4. See Luke 11:2

Chapter 11: My Heart is Past Sick
1. See Joshua 6:1-3
2. See Joshua 6:10
3. See 2 Corinthians 4:8-9
4. See Romans 8:28
5. See Isaiah 55:8-9
6. See 1 Peter 5:7
7. See Philippians 4:6
8. See Hebrews 11:1
9. See Proverbs 13:12
10. See Psalm 18:10
11. See Psalm 18:13
12. See Jonah 2:5
13. See 1 Peter 5:10 (HCSB)
14. See John 10:10
15. See Job 33 and on (Elihu Confronts Job)
16. See Revelation 4:11, John 1:3
17. See Job 34:13
18. See Job 38:4
19. See Job 34:12

20. See Job 34:29
21. See Deuteronomy 32:4

Chapter 12: Claiming a Dependent
1. See Hebrews 3:6
2. See Psalm 62:7, Isaiah 26:3, 2 Chronicles 14:11
3. See Philippians 4:19, Psalm 104:14-15
4. See 1 John 1:7, John 13:8
5. See Psalm 32:8, Psalm 24:8, John 14:6
6. See Psalm 91:14
7. See Psalm 41:3 (NASB), Matthew 4:23-24, Psalm 103:3, James 5:14-15
8. See Psalm 147:3, Ezekiel 34:16
9. See Psalm 4:8
10. See 2 Corinthians 1:22
11. See Job 34:14-15, John 15:5
12. Hawks, Annie S. "I Need Thee Every Hour". Ref by Robert, Lowry. 1872.
13. See John 14:2-3

Chapter 13: My Purpose
1. See Job 7:7 (NASB)
2. See Galatians 5:22-23
3. See Psalm 145:9
4. See Matthew 18:12-14
5. See Ephesians 1:4-6, 1 John 4:19, Romans 8:38-39
6. See Isaiah 43:21, 1 Peter 2:9
7. See Ephesians 2:10
8. See Psalm 139:13
9. See 1 Corinthians 12:4-7 (NASB)
10. See 2 Peter 1:3, 2 Timothy 3:16-17
11. See John 15:16-19
12. See 2 Chronicles 23:1

Chapter 14: Music
1. See Psalm 148:7-13, Psalm 98:4-9, Psalm 96:11-13
2. Kammermeier, Laura. "Birds of the World Species Profiles - and a Special Offer." eBird, 10 August 2020, https://ebird.org/news/birds-of-the-world-species-pro-files.
3. See Genesis 1:3
4. See Revelation 1:10-13 (NASB)
5. See Psalm 81:1-3, Psalm 150:3-6, 2 Chronicles 5:12-13
6. See 1 Chronicles 13:8
7. See 2 Chronicles 30:21
8. See Acts 16:25 (NASB)
9. See Luke 15:25
10. See Revelation 5:8-9

11. See Psalm 51:10, Psalm 71:23
12. See Revelation 19:6
13. See 2 Samuel 22:4, Revelation 5:11-12
14. Crosby, Frances J. "Blessed Assurance". 1873.

Chapter 15: The Grass
1. See Psalm 19:1, Romans 8:28
2. See Malachi 2:10, Colossians 1:16
3. See Isaiah 40:6
4. See Psalm 115:16
5. See Genesis 2:7, Job 12:10
6. See 2 Corinthians 4:16
7. See Romans 8:10-11, 1 John 3:14
8. See John 4:14, 1 John 1:5-7
9. See Galatians 3:27-28
10. See Ephesians 6:12
11. See Psalm 31:5, John 15:26
12. See 1 Samuel 16:7 (NASB)

Chapter 16: The Guilty
1. See 1 Samuel 16:7 (NASB)
2. See Genesis 2:7
3. See Psalm 139:14 (NASB)
4. See Titus 3:3
5. See Isaiah 53:5, Mark 15:37-39 (NASB)
6. See Romans 5:8
7. See Romans 5:10
8. See Deuteronomy 10:17-18
9. See Romans 15:33
10. See 1 John 4:8
11. See Revelation 22:16
12. See Colossians 3:12-13
13. See Leviticus 19:17 (NASB), Proverbs 24:17-18
14. See Ephesians 2:4-5
15. See Matthew 25:34, Matthew 27:37

Chapter 17: The Fight
1. See Genesis 3:1
2. See John 16:33 (NASB)
3. See Revelation 20:10
4. See 2 Timothy 1:7, Acts 1:8
5. See Proverbs 28:1
6. See Psalm 91:5-8 (NASB)
7. See 2 Samuel 22:7
8. See Psalm 18:10
9. See Psalm 18:14
10. See Psalm 18:8

11. See James 1:5
12. See Romans 8:26

Chapter 18: The Course
1. See 2 Corinthians 11:14
2. See John 8:44
3. See Ephesians 6:11
4. See Revelation 2:24
5. See Romans 10:9
6. See Ephesians 6:16
7. See 1 Corinthians 12:27, Colossians 1:18
8. See 1 Peter 3:8
9. See Romans 12:16
10. See Isaiah 55:9
11. See Romans 14:13, Leviticus 19:14
12. See Romans 6:13
13. See Romans 12:10
14. See Romans 12:17
15. See Romans 12:18
16. See 2 Timothy 2:24-25
17. See Luke 6:27
18. See Luke 6:28
19. See Romans 12:20
20. See Leviticus 19:18
21. See Matthew 12:30
22. See 1 Timothy 2:1-2
23. See Matthew 5:44
24. See Ephesians 6:18
25. See Romans 12:2
26. See Ephesians 5:11
27. See Zephaniah 2:3
28. See Deuteronomy 11:18
29. See Exodus 20:3
30. See Exodus 34:14
31. See Matthew 22:36-39 (NASB)
32. See Psalm 103:2-5
33. See Job 34:14-15
34. See Psalm 83:3
35. See 1 Thessalonians 5:21, Hebrews 3:6, Matthew 10:22
36. See John 14:6
37. See Matthew 25:46

Chapter 19: Questions
1. See Genesis 2:7
2. See Genesis 6:19
3. See Mark 16:15
4. See 1 John 4:8

5. See Mark 8:6-9
6. See Luke 9:13-14 (NASB)
7. See Genesis 1:20-25 (HCSB)
8. See Genesis 2:19
9. See 1 John 1:5
10. See Revelation 4:5
11. See Habakkuk 3:4
12. See Mark 16:15
13. See 2 Corinthians 5:20
14. See 1 Corinthians 12:5
15. See Genesis 9:2
16. See Luke 10:19
17. Ramel, Gordon. "The Insect Abdomen: Guide To The Digestive & Reproductive Systems". Earth Life, https://www.earthlife.net/insects/anat-abdomen.html.
18. See John 1:18, John 10:30
19. See Matthew 2:1-2
20. See John 8:6-8 (NASB)
21. See Mark 5:13
22. See Matthew 27:52-53 (NASB)
23. See John 1:36
24. See Luke 3:22
25. See Romans 15:12-13 (NASB), 1 Peter 1:3, Matthew 12:21, 1 Timothy 1:1
26. See Ezekiel 1:28, Revelation 4:3
27. See 1 John 1:5
28. See Revelation 8:1
29. See Revelation 22:1-2 (NASB)
30. See Revelation 21:1 (NASB)
31. See Revelation 22:5, Revelation 21:23, Isaiah 60:19-20
32. See Revelation 22:2
33. See John 20:31
34. See Genesis 7:11-12 (NASB)
35. See Revelation 8:6
36. See Revelation 19:11
37. See Matthew 22:30
38. See Acts 3:21
39. See Revelation 21:1 (NASB)
40. See Genesis 2:22-24
41. See Ephesians 6:17, Hebrews 4:12 (NASB)
42. See Psalm 139:16

Chapter 20: Comparison
1. See 2 Corinthians 6:18
2. See Psalm 4:3
3. See James 1:17, Matthew 7:11
4. See Jeremiah 29:11
5. See Luke 1:37

6. See Psalm 139:14 (NASB)
7. See 1 John 5:3-5
8. See Mark 16:15

Chapter 21: Sustainment
1. See Matthew 8:24
2. See Matthew 14:24
3. See Mark 4:38-39
4. See John 21:5-6 (NASB)

Chapter 22: Thank You Friend
1. See Proverbs 27:17
2. See Acts 17:25

Chapter 23: Kicking Down the Wall for You
1. John 15:9, Proverbs 8:17
2. See Isaiah 61:1-3 (HCSB)
3. See John 8:44, Revelation 20:10
4. See 2 Kings 6:16 (NASB)

Chapter 24: Always Enough
1. See Genesis 2:20 (NASB)
2. See Psalm 100:3
3. See Genesis 2:7
4. See Luke 19:10, Matthew 18:12
5. See Mark 15:37 (NASB)
6. See John 15:19
7. See Genesis 1:31
8. See 1 Peter 3:3-4 (NASB)
9. See 2 Corinthians 2:15
10. See Proverbs 12:4

Chapter 25: Out of the Valley
1. See Job 42:12
2. See Genesis 41:39-41 (NASB)
3. See Romans 8:28
4. See Isaiah 61:3 (HCSB)
5. See Psalm 34:18
6. See 1 Peter 2:24, Psalm 107:20
7. See 2 Corinthians 1:3
8. See John 13:13, Isaiah 30:20-21 (NASB)
9. See 1 John 1:9
10. See Luke 12:29-31, Philippians 4:19
11. See 1 Peter 5:10
12. See 2 Thessalonians 3:16
13. See Exodus 3:14
14. See Matthew 6:13 (NASB)

Chapter 26: Diamonds Part 1
1. See John 8:12
2. See Psalm 118:24
3. See Ephesians 4:15
4. See Romans 12:2 (NASB), Ephesians 4:20-24 (NASB)
5. See Colossians 3:2
6. See Romans 12:2 (NASB)
7. See 2 Timothy 1:7
8. See Hebrews 13:9, 2 Peter 3:17
9. See Romans 12:2 (NASB)
10. See Ephesians 6:12
11. See Mark 12:28-31 (NASB), John 13:34-35, Luke 6:27-28
12. See 1 John 3:18
13. See 2 Timothy 3:16-17
14. See 1 Thessalonians 5:11, Hebrews 10:25 (NASB)
15. See Psalm 118:24
16. See Ephesians 4:15
17. See Romans 6:13
18. See 2 Timothy 2:3
19. Lemmel, Helen H. "Turn Your Eyes upon Jesus". 1922.

Chapter 26: Diamonds Part 2
1. See 1 John 4:8
2. See Matthew 5:44
3. See 1 Timothy 2:1-2
4. See Ephesians 6:18
5. See Job 33:4 (NASB)
6. See Luke 6:27
7. See Proverbs 24:17
8. See Romans 12:19
9. See Romans 12:10
10. See John 10:27
11. See Proverbs 15:1
12. See Romans 12:18
13. See Romans 12:21
14. See Acts 2:20
15. Lemmel, Helen H. "Turn Your Eyes upon Jesus". 1922.

Chapter 27: He is Good
1. See Psalm 40:2
2. See Isaiah 43:16
3. See Psalm 121:3 (NASB)
4. See Psalm 18:19
5. See Genesis 2:7
6. See John 15:19

7. See Psalm 4:3
8. See Mark 15:37 (NASB)
9. See John 3:16
10. See John 3:16
11. See Psalm 139:16

Chapter 28: Keep Going
1. Lewis, Shari. "The Song That Doesn't End". Lamb Chop's Sing-Along, Play-Along. By Shari Lewis. 1992.
2. See John 10:10
3. See 1 Kings 19:7
4. See Deuteronomy 6:3, Revelation 21:1-4 (NASB)
5. See Ephesians 6:11
6. See 2 Timothy 1:7, Acts 1:8
7. See John 12:1
8. See Luke 11:9
9. See 1 John 4:17
10. See 2 Corinthians 1:8
11. See Mark 14:34 (HCSB)
12. See 2 Corinthians 4:17

Chapter 29: Out at Sea
1. See Acts 1:8
2. See Matthew 17:20
3. See 2 Kings 2:8

Chapter 30: Loneliness
1. See Matthew 28:20
2. See Proverbs 15:3

Chapter 31: The Woods
1. See Psalm 55:6-7
2. See Ezekiel 20:6
3. See Exodus 13:21
4. See Exodus 16:4
5. See Philippians 4:5
6. See Psalm 100:3
7. See Numbers 20:8
8. See Isaiah 41:13
9. See Psalm 23:3
10. See Psalm 23:6 (KJV)
11. See Exodus 13:21
12. See Psalm 91:4
13. See Psalm 34:7
14. See Psalm 4:8
15. See Philippians 4:7
16. See Psalm 91:4

17. See Exodus 14:2

Chapter 32: Game Over
1. See Matthew 16:18 (KJV)

Chapter 33: Future Life
1. See John 4:14, John 7:38-39 (NASB)
2. See John 8:12, 2 Corinthians 4:6
3. See Ephesians 6:10
4. See John 11:25
5. See John 14:6
6. See Colossians 2:6-7
7. See Psalm 100:5
8. See John 1:16
9. See 2 Peter 3:18
10. See John 10:10
11. See James 5:11

Chapter 34: What Jesus Says
1. See Psalm 145:9
2. See Psalm 119:64
3. FREESTORIESANDGAMES. "Top Ten Most Mentioned Animals in the Bible". Free stories and games WordPress, 14 November 2017, https://freestoriesand-games.wordpress.com/2017/11/14/top-ten-most-mentioned-animals-in-the-bi-ble/.
   Reasons for Hope* Jesus. "Animals in the Bible". Reasons for Hope Jesus, 6 July 2016, https://reasonsforhopejesus.com/fun-facts-animals-bible/.
4. See Genesis 1:21, Genesis 1:25
5. See Luke 12:6
6. See Psalm 104:14
7. See Psalm 104:10-11
8. See Psalm 104:21
9. See Job 38:41
10. See Psalm 104:27-28
11. See Psalm 145:16
12. See Psalm 36:6 (NASB)
13. See Genesis 6:19
14. See Genesis 9:15-16
15. See Psalm 50:10-11
16. See Proverbs 12:10 (HCSB)
17. See Proverbs 27:23
18. See Deuteronomy 22:4
19. See Exodus 23:5
20. See Leviticus 22:27
21. See Jonah 4:11
22. See Exodus 23:12
23. See John 10:27

24. See Isaiah 40:11
25. See Proverbs 6:6-9 (NASB)
26. See Jeremiah 8:7
27. See Numbers 22:28
28. See Jonah 1:17 (NASB)
29. See 1 Kings 17:4-6 (NASB)
30. See Leviticus 24:18
31. See Psalm 17:8
32. See Deuteronomy 32:11
33. See John 1:29
34. See Luke 3:22
35. See Isaiah 43:20
36. See Job 12:7-9
37. See 2 Kings 6:17 (NASB)
38. See Isaiah 11:6-7 (HCSB)
39. See Revelation 5:13
40. See Romans 8:19, Romans 8:23
41. See Revelation 5:5
42. See Revelation 19:11
43. See Revelation 19:14
44. Watts, Isaac. "Joy to the World". 1719.

Chapter 35: My Baby
1. See Job 34:14-15
2. See James 1:17
3. See Psalm 24:1
4. See Revelation 5:13

Chapter 36: Partners Not in Crime
1. See John 8:44, Revelation 20:10
2. See Mark 16:15
3. See 1 Peter 4:10
4. See Matthew 13:45-46
5. See Psalm 83:3
6. See 1 Corinthians 12:27, Ephesians 4:15-16
7. See 1 Thessalonians 5:11
8. See Ephesians 6:18
9. See 2 Corinthians 1:7, 1 Peter 5:9
10. See Hebrews 12:1
11. See Psalm 107:14-16 (HCSB)
12. See John 8:44

Chapter 37: Helping Animals
1. See 1 Corinthians 12:4-5 (NASB)
2. See 1 Peter 4:10
3. See Colossians 1:18, 1 Corinthians 12:27
4. See Daniel 2:22 (NASB)

5. Organization name used by the permission of Animal Recovery Mission.
6. See Psalm 145:9
7. See John 14:26
8. See Mark 16:15
9. See John 13:34-35
10. See 1 Corinthians 3:9
11. See 1 Corinthians 3:9
12. See Romans 6:13
13. See Proverbs 12:10 (HCSB)
14. See Proverbs 12:10 (HCSB)
15. "Don't Feed Ducks and Geese Bread; You're Making Them Sick". Reconnect with Nature, 4 March 2021, https://www.reconnectwithnature.org/news-events/the-buzz/dont-feed-ducks-geese-bread.
16. "Migratory Bird Treaty Act". U.S. Fish & Wildlife Service, https://www.fws.gov/birds/policies-and-regulations/laws-legislations/migratory-bird-treaty-act.php.
17. "Birds 101". cfwinterns, 4 March 2011, https://cfwinterns.wordpress.com/tag/ornithology/.
18. See Ezekiel 36:26-27

Chapter 38: Those Unsure of Jesus
1. See 3 John 1:7
2. See 1 Peter 3:15
3. See John 3:16
4. See 1 John 3:1, John 14:17
5. See Matthew 5:48
6. See Hebrews 4:12 (NASB)
7. See 1 John 4:7-11, John 3:16, John 15:9
8. See Colossians 1:16
9. See Genesis 1:27
10. See Genesis 2:7, Job 33:4 (NASB)
11. See Genesis 3 (The Temptation and the Fall)
12. See Genesis 3:14-19, Romans 8:20-22
13. See Isaiah 59:2
14. See Galatians 4:4-5, John 6:38
15. See 1 Timothy 3:16, Philippians 2:5-8
16. See Isaiah 53:4-6, Romans 3:23
17. See Ephesians 2:8-9, Romans 6:23
18. See John 3:16
19. See Mark 10:34, Mark 16:6, 1 Corinthians 15:3-4
20. See Acts 2:24
21. See Matthew 4:17, John 1:12, Ephesians 2:19
22. See Romans 3:23-26 (NASB)
23. See Acts 4:11-12, John 14:6
24. See 1 Corinthians 15:4-8
25. See Acts 1:9-11, John 16:7-11
26. See Romans 16:25-27

27. See Matthew 16:27, John 14:3, Hebrews 9:28
28. See Mark 13:26-27, Romans 5:19
29. See Revelation 20:10
30. See Matthew 11:29 (NASB)
31. See Luke 1:49, Deuteronomy 10:17
32. See 1 Peter 5:7, Psalm 145:9, Psalm 144:3
33. See Psalm 139:16
34. See Jeremiah 1:5, Isaiah 44:24
35. See Genesis 2:7, Job 33:4 (NASB)
36. See Isaiah 45:5
37. See Psalm 139:14 (NASB)
38. See Matthew 18:12-14
39. See Matthew 28:20, Joshua 1:9
40. See 2 Peter 3:9, 1 Timothy 2:3-4
41. See Matthew 22:8-10 (HCSB)

Chapter 40: The Two Lines
1. See Philippians 4:7
2. See Matthew 7:13-14
3. See Proverbs 14:12
4. See Matthew 4:19 (NASB)
5. See Hebrews 13:6, John 14:16 (NASB)
6. See Philippians 4:19
7. See 1 Corinthians 2:14
8. See Romans 5:8-10, Acts 2:23-24
9. See 2 Peter 3:3
10. See Galatians 5:22
11. See Psalm 4:3, 2 Timothy 2:21
12. See Matthew 4:17, See Matthew 10:7
13. See Proverbs 14:12
14. See John 14:6
15. See Mark 4:9
16. See 1 Corinthians 15:3-4, 1 Peter 2:24, Romans 4:24-25 (NASB)
17. See Acts 1:11
18. See Romans 10:9
19. See Job 12:7-9
20. See Romans 6:23
21. See Revelation 22:12, 2 Timothy 4:18, Colossians 1:13
22. See Titus 2:14, Psalm 19:14

Chapter 41: Epic God
1. See Genesis 1:1
2. See Genesis 1:2, John 1:1-2
3. See Acts 17:28 (NASB)
4. See Isaiah 40:22
5. See Psalm 19:1
6. See Psalm 147:4

7. See Acts 17:25
8. See Jeremiah 23:23-24 (NASB)
9. See Matthew 19:26
10. See Colossians 1:15-17, John 1:3, Revelation 4:11
11. See John 8:44
12. See John 8:44
13. See 2 Corinthians 11:14
14. See Genesis 3:13, 2 Corinthians 11:3
15. See John 6:19, John 11:43-44, Acts 2:24
16. See Philippians 2:5-8
17. See Hebrews 13:8, Job 23:13
18. See Matthew 1:20-21, John 1:41-42
19. See Colossians 3:14, 1 John 4:8
20. See Colossians 3:17
21. See Exodus 3:14
22. See Colossians 1:18
23. See Philippians 2:9-11, Isaiah 40:26, Job 38:31-32 (NASB)
24. See John 8:42, John 6:38, John 3:13
25. See Ephesians 6:11-12
26. See Acts 10:36, Colossians 1:17-18, Revelation 17:14
27. See Hebrews 1:3, Hebrews 11:3, Psalm 33:6
28. See Hebrews 4:12 (NASB)
29. See Ephesians 6:17, Hebrews 4:12 (NASB)
30. See Psalm 18:10
31. See Jeremiah 48:40
32. See Psalm 29:7
33. See Deuteronomy 4:24
34. See Psalm 108:13
35. See Psalm 11:6
36. See Psalm 11:6
37. See Joshua 10:10, Exodus 14:24-25, Exodus 23:27,
    1 Samuel 7:10
38. See Judges 7:22
39. See Jeremiah 4:11-13
40. See 1 Peter 2:24, Isaiah 53:5
41. See Hebrews 12:25, 2 Thessalonians 1:8-9, 1 Peter 4:17,
    Isaiah 1:20
42. See Romans 8:10-11, Ephesians 2:4-5
43. See Acts 2:24
44. See Mark 15:37 (NASB)
45. See Revelation 1:17-18
46. See Colossians 1:18
47. See John 3:16, Luke 24:2-3, John 11:43-44, Matthew 27:50-53 (NASB)
48. See Revelation 3:14
49. See Mark 9:31, John 14:3
50. See 1 Corinthians 15:3-4, Acts 1:11, Revelation 22:12
51. See Matthew 12:30 (NASB)

52. See Romans 10:9
53. See Proverbs 4:20-22, Proverbs 3:7-8
54. See Proverbs 4:9
55. See Psalm 31:24, Psalm 27:3, Psalm 112:7
56. See Exodus 34:6, Psalm 42:8
57. See Psalm 86:5, Ephesians 2:7
58. See Psalm 103:8
59. See Psalm 86:15, Ephesians 2:6-8
60. See Genesis 3:21
61. See Genesis 6:13-17
62. See Genesis 21:1-2, 1 Samuel 1:20, Judges 13:3 (NASB), Luke 1:13 (NASB)
63. See Genesis 41:39-41 (NASB)
64. See Exodus 7:3-4
65. See Exodus 15:24, Exodus 16:4, Exodus 16:11-12, Numbers 20:11
66. See Exodus 14:16, Joshua 3:13, 2 Kings 2:14
67. See Daniel 3:19
68. See Judges 14:5-6 (NASB)
69. See Daniel 6:22-23
70. See 1 Samuel 17:17
71. See Psalm 91:11
72. See Lamentations 3:22-23
73. See Jonah 1:17 (NASB)
74. See Psalm 147:3, Isaiah 53:4-5, Matthew 4:23
75. See John 21:5-6 (NASB)
76. See John 14:26
77. See Psalm 46:1, Philippians 4:13, Isaiah 40:29-31
78. See Psalm 107:13-16
79. See Acts 16:25-34 (NASB)
80. See Isaiah 43:16, Acts 2:22, Numbers 23:19, 2 Corinthians 4:6, SINACH. "Way Maker." Way Maker (Live). By SINACH, 2016.
81. See Psalm 83:3
82. See 2 Peter 3:13
83. See Revelation 16:14, Revelation 19:19, 2 Timothy 2:3-4 (NASB)
84. See Romans 13:12
85. See Revelation 20:7-9
86. See Joel 2:11
87. See Matthew 10:34
88. See Exodus 15:3 (HCSB)
89. See Isaiah 63:1 (NASB), Zephaniah 3:17
90. See John 14:30
91. See Revelation 5:11-12
92. See Revelation 6:14
93. See Joel 3:16
94. See Joel 3:16
95. See Luke 8:25
96. See Psalm 104:26-27

97. See Hebrews 4:13
98. See Proverbs 15:3
99. See Job 34:14-15
100. See Revelation 20:10
101. See Zephaniah 1:14
102. See Revelation 19:11-14
103. See Revelation 20:10
104. See 2 Thessalonians 1:8-9 (HCSB)
105. See Matthew 13:41-42, Luke 13:27-28, Daniel 12:2,
    Revelation 14:9-11
106. See Revelation 19:2
107. See Revelation 5:13 (NASB)
108. See Revelation 5:13 (NASB)
109. See Revelation 21:6
110. See Revelation 7:9-10 (HCSB)
111. See Ecclesiastes 12:13

Chapter 42: Those Enduring to the End

1. See 1 John 5:19
2. See John 8:44
3. See Revelation 18:23
4. See John 10:10
5. See John 14:6, Romans 3:4
6. See John 15:18-19 (NASB)
7. See Matthew 22:37
8. See Matthew 7:14, Mark 4:9
9. See Matthew 7:13
10. See James 1:5
11. See Genesis 3:1
12. See 1 Corinthians 12:4 (NASB), 1 Corinthians 12:13 (NASB)
13. See Matthew 25:8
14. See John 15:19
15. See Revelation 1:3
16. See Matthew 22:2
17. See 2 Chronicles 30:8, Jeremiah 10:10
18. See Matthew 22:11-12, Revelation 3:5
19. See Revelation 14:13
20. See Revelation 3:11 (NASB)
21. See Acts 4:11
22. See Mark 13:31, Psalm 145:13, 1 John 2:17
23. See John 5:24, John 5:28-29, John 11:25
24. See Revelation 1:18
25. See Hebrews 13:5 (KJV), Deuteronomy 31:6 (KJV)
26. See Revelation 21:27
27. See Psalm 37:29, Daniel 12:1-2, Matthew 13:40-43
28. See Revelation 19:16
29. See Matthew 24:13, Revelation 14:12

ABOUT
KHARIS PUBLISHING

KHARIS PUBLISHING is an independent, traditional publishing house with a core mission to publish impactful books, and channel proceeds into establishing mini-libraries or resource centers for orphanages in developing countries, so these kids will learn to read, dream, and grow. Every time you purchase a book from Kharis Publishing or partner as an author, you are helping give these kids an amazing opportunity to read, dream, and grow. Kharis Publishing is an imprint of Kharis Media LLC. Learn more at https://www.kharispublishing.com.